WHEN HE APPEARS

CHRIST'S FINAL STEPS IN PREPARING US FOR HIS COMING

WHEN HE
APPEARS

CHRIST'S FINAL STEPS IN
PREPARING US FOR HIS COMING

RON AUCH

New Leaf Press

First printing: August 2000

ISBN: 0-89221-498-8
Library of Congress Number: 00-102660

Cover by Left Coast Design, Portland, OR.

Printed in the United States of America.

Please visit our website for other great titles:
www.newleafpress.net

For information regarding publicity for author interviews contact Dianna Fletcher at (870) 438-5288.

This book is dedicated to all those who seek the "separated life" and are doing all they can to prepare themselves for when He appears!

WHEN HE APPEARS

Dear friends, now we are children of God,
and what we will be has not yet been
made known. But we know that *when he
appears,* we shall be like him, for we shall
see him as he is (1 John 3:2;NIV).

CONTENTS

INTRODUCTION

W*hen He Appears* uses the Song of Solomon as its backdrop. For many years I have been fascinated with this most arresting book. It reveals the deep need for an intimate relationship with Christ and our need to prepare for His soon coming more so than any other book in the Bible.

The Bible is very clear about the fact that our Lord is coming back for us one day. It seems one of the most overlooked aspects of His return is our own preparation for it. The Song of Songs not only shows us the great length our Lord has gone to win our hearts, it also reveals His continual work in preparing us to be a bride without spot or wrinkle. Jesus is coming for a bride that is ready and waiting for Him. Let's be that bride!

I have had several influences concerning this book: The Holy Spirit, *Queen of the Realm* (currently out of print) by Rev. Delmer R. Guynes, and *The Secret of the Stairs* by Rev. Wade Taylor. I will be using *Queen of the Realm* as the basic premise for this book.

Rev. Guynes states in the introduction of his book:

> Jesus often spoke in parables. These were
> stories from human life that revealed and

sometimes concealed spiritual truths. Someone has suggested that they were "earthly stories with heavenly meanings." The Song of Solomon is such a story. It is, in fact, a love song or perhaps a dramatic play or operatic presentation written in celebration of Solomon's first and perhaps only true love, his love for a maiden from the village of Shunem (Shulem) in lower Galilee near the valley of Jesreel. Solomon was a poet and writer-collector of wise sayings, proverbs, and songs. This love song to the Shunammite girl was written for him or by him, and possibly was in celebration of their marriage, as would be customary.

The Song of Solomon cannot be read like a western love story or novel. Its structure is oriental, somewhat like a Chinese opera or shadow play. The meaning or plot has to be discovered by listening to a wide range of episodes which reveal and illustrate various aspects of the story. These are not necessarily reported in the sequence in which they occurred.[1]

Guynes goes on to say that the book was probably written after Solomon and Abishag (the Shulamite) were married. The book is a reflection of their courtship. It is a "looking back" at the wonderful and mysterious events surrounding this most riveting relationship.

The Song, or opera, with its 13 canticles (verses or episodes) seems to be a hodge-podge of experiences. Some are in the present, some are flashbacks, some are dreams and some are fantasies that young people in love might experience. The movement occurs more like a dream would unfold, with sudden bursts of events that may seem unrelated but when taken all together form a kaleidoscope of events that tells an entire story. The Song would be understood more easily if all the vignettes or episodes could be seen as the physical and emotional experiences, over a period of several years, of two young people very much in love, looking forward to and eventually experiencing ecstatic marriage.[2]

To some, the Song of Solomon should not even be in the Bible. By Christian standards it is suggestive and, if taken literally, teaches a loose or liberal view of a love relationship between a king and his paramour. This comes from a lack of understanding the intimacy Christ (the King) longs to have with His bride (the Church). To suggest that some of the language in the "Song" should not be there is to assume a purity that exceeds God's. We are not more pure than God. The Book of Titus says: To the pure, all things are pure; but to those who are defiled and unbelieving, nothing is pure, but both their mind and their conscience are defiled (Titus 1:15).

It is only the impure heart that would have a perverted focus concerning this book. The Holy Spirit wants us to understand the spiritual truths in this book. If we think that some of it should not be there we exalt ourselves above God himself.

TYPOLOGY

Some may struggle with an allegorical look at this book. Many believe we cannot read anything into the story at all. They believe it's simply the account of Solomon and his bride. While it is true that it is their story, there is much more to be gained from it than just historical facts. The revelation of most biblical truths are gained through typology or allegories. The whole typology of Scripture is founded upon a law of mutual resemblance. In other words,

Scripture interprets Scripture. The study of Scripture reveals that each aspect of the Divine can be perfectly combined with every other aspect.

The apostle Paul used allegories to make many important points. Galatians 4:24 states: "This is allegorically speaking: for these {women} are two covenants, one {proceeding} from Mount Sinai bearing children who are to be slaves; she is Hagar." Paul uses these two women as examples (types) of the two covenants.

Thomas Bernard says, "It was of high importance to the clearness and fixedness of the doctrine, that this connection between the two covenants should be deliberately shown to consist not in rhetorical illustration, but in a divinely intended system of analogies."[3]

In 1 Corinthians 10:6 we read, "Now these things happened as examples [types] for us." Paul does not treat this as an event that first occurred, and then found afterward it conveyed a useful lesson. He boldly asserts that this event was an "intent of God," which was allowed to happen specifically for the lesson's sake. This is its purpose for being recorded in the Scriptures.

Guynes states, "Some of what I have suggested is conjecture, and nowhere in Scripture is this interpretation fully presented. However, as I viewed the Song of Solomon from this perspective, the Book suddenly took on cohesive meaning. It became to me the great Old Testament parable of the grace of God that could take a despised and abused young maiden and, through a series of both painful and exhilarating experiences, bring her from obscurity to the position of Queen of the Realm."[4]

Solomon ended up having many wives and many concubines. This probably contributed largely to the confused state of mind he expresses in the Book of Ecclesiastes. In Ecclesiastes 2:10 he says, "And all that my eyes desired I did not refuse them. I did not withhold my heart from any pleasure, for my heart was pleased because of all my labor and this was my reward for all my labor."

It's hard for the average person to fathom what it would be like to be able to have anything our hearts desire. Solomon could. It's very possible that if we had the same option we would follow the same path he did.

> The Song of Solomon was Solomon's tribute to his first and probably only true love. Later, Solomon married for political reasons and took many concubines. His life became debauched and lost the blessing of God. But in those early years of Solomon's kingship, God seems to have allowed him and Abishag to live out a romance so beautiful and pure, though in sordid surroundings, that it pleased the Holy Spirit to let it be included in the text of Scripture as a magnificent illustration of the intended love relationship between the Father and Israel and Jesus and His Church.[5]

WHAT'S NOT TO UNDERSTAND?

"Have you not read?" was the usual query of Jesus in drawing profound inferences from the simplest statements. His words imply, "Have you not read it thus? You also should have seen its meaning as I do. How is it you do not understand?" There has been a great neglect of the types in the church. It's possible that this can be traced to the fact that understanding types requires a spiritual intelligence that many Christians lack.

Jesus could also have said, "Do you not have any spiritual disciplines in your life? If you did, you too would understand what you have read just as I do." Insight requires a certain measure of spiritual capacity that comes through habitual exercise in the things of God. Not many possess insight because they lack a deep desire to fellowship with Jesus. To understand the Song of Solomon in its fullness, there must be a longing for Jesus. There must be a deep desire in your life expressed through a prayer similar to the bride's as she says, "Draw me, Lord!"

There is a great lack of longing for Jesus in the church today. This is expressed in the "Song" through the group of people called the "daughters of Zion." The "daughters" are also called the "friends" or the "watchmen." They are the ones that serve God from a distance. They do not understand intimacy. They do not want intimacy. Subsequently, they do not practice the spiritual disciplines necessary to develop the ability to "see" spiritually.

I trust you will see what it is God has for you in this wonderful book. It is also my prayer that you will develop all the disciplines necessary to "behold" the Shepherd of your soul.

CHAPTER ONE

THE CHARACTERS

To fully appreciate this wonderful book we must first understand its main characters. The "Song" has many personalities, but the two most important are the bride and the groom. There are other characters as well, such as King David, Solomon's stepbrother Adonijah, and the daughters of Zion, who are the friends of the bride. It will be important for us to come into a full understanding of who these characters are if we are to grasp the fullness of this book.

> Now King David was old, advanced in age; and they covered him with clothes, but he could not keep warm. So his servants said to him, "Let them seek a young virgin for my lord the king, and let her attend the king and become his nurse; and let her lie in your bosom, that my lord the king may keep warm." So they searched for a beautiful girl throughout all the territory of Israel, and found Abishag the Shunammite, and brought her to the king. The girl was very beautiful; and she became the king's nurse and served him, but the king did not cohabit with her (1 Kings 1:1–4).

THE BRIDE

One day I was reading in 1 Kings 1 and 2 the story of Abishag, the Shunammite maiden, who was brought to Jerusalem to be King David's concubine. The relationship was never consummated, but in the time frame of Abishag's stay at Jerusalem, both Solomon and Adonijah, contenders for the throne, fell in love with her.

I realized then that Abishag, from the village of Shunem of 1 Kings chapters 1 and 2, might well be the Shulamite of the Song of Solomon. The sounds for "n" and "l" in many oriental languages are hard to distinguish, and in transliteration can be interchanged easily. In my opinion, Shunem and Shulem are slightly different spellings for the same place, which often occurs in the recording of names of biblical places.

Shunem or Shulem was in the area of lower Galilee in the high foothills of the mountains of Lebanon. King David and King Solomon owned large estates there with vineyards, spice gardens, and fruit orchards. The vast sheep herds of the royal family were kept here. These farmlands and flocks were cared for by tenants who were paid from the king's treasury.

Abishag was a daughter in one of these tenant families. Scripture indicates that she was brought to Jerusalem to become a concubine to King David, probably against her will. Providentially, she became only a servant maiden to David, the relationship never being consummated. She faithfully tended to David in his waning years and it was during that time she became the object of affection for both Solomon and Adonijah.[1]

After King David died, Abishag was sent back to her home. This would have been a very difficult thing for her family to deal with. It would have been a great honor for any family to have one of their members serving in the inner court of the king. It certainly would have meant all types of favors for the family, including financial ones.

When Abishag returned home, she was disgraced. Though David did not cohabit with Abishag, she would have been looked upon as one of the king's concubines. How could she convince her neighbors that she merely served the king? In Song of Solomon 1:5 she expresses a bit of her dilemma:

> "I am black but lovely, O daughters of Jerusalem, Like the tents of Kedar, Like the curtains of Solomon."

She asserts her own inner beauty but because man looks on the outside, she feels soiled outwardly. When she says, "I am black," she is referring to how she feels outwardly. She compares herself to the tents of Kedar, in which the shepherds lived, which were very coarse and never whitened, weather-beaten, and discolored by long use.

Then she adds, "But lovely . . . like the curtains of Solomon," the furniture of whose rooms, no doubt, was sumptuous and rich, in proportion to the stateliness of his houses. The Church is sometimes black in the eyes of the world, but comely in God's esteem. Abishag knows her own heart. She knows she has done no wrong despite what the world around her may think.

The king's former nurse had good reason to think the whole world was against her because of the rejection of her own household. In verse 6 we read:

> "Do not stare at me because I am swarthy,
> For the sun has burned me. My mother's sons

were angry with me; They made me caretaker of the vineyards, {But} I have not taken care of my own vineyard."

When she calls herself "swarthy" she is not referring to her skin color. She is simply expressing that she feels black and dirty from working out in the hot sun. When she came back from the king's court, her own brothers turned on her and gave her the menial task of working the vineyard. She says, "Do not stare at me." Abishag could just as easily have said, "Do not look to me as an example." She feels hypocritical. She is tending her brother's vineyards while failing to tend her own. In the midst of these conflicting thoughts about herself, she finds herself attracted to a mysterious young shepherd who has expressed an interest in her. He is working the field next to hers.

THE ADVERSARY

Before we can continue with the love story of Solomon and Abishag, we must factor in Solomon's stepbrother Adonijah. There is no mention of Adonijah in the "Song" itself. We read of him in the book of 1 Kings. The only other mention of his name in the entire Word of God is in various genealogies. God has a very important message to bring to us through him. Adonijah is a type of our unscrupulous adversary, Satan. He represents the enemy's desire to dethrone the King through attaining His bride.

In 1 Kings 1 we read of King David's last days. Abishag was brought in to console the king. In verse 4 we read:

> The girl was very beautiful; and she became the king's nurse and served him, but the king did not cohabit with her.

It seems that both Solomon and Adonijah fell in love with Abishag while she served their ailing father. Though

Solomon and Adonijah shared a father, they did not share the same mother. Solomon was born to Bathsheba while Adonijah's mother was Haggith. It seems they did not share the typical "brotherly" relationship many of us might be used to. Theirs was more professional. This would not be abnormal among royalty where political maneuvering might mean saving your life.

It eventually became obvious that King David would not live much longer. At that time Adonijah abandoned any pursuit of Abishag, preferring the kingship instead. In 1 Kings 1:5 we read:

> Now Adonijah the son of Haggith exalted himself, saying, "I will be king." So he prepared for himself chariots and horsemen with fifty men to run before him.

> Well, this caused quite a stir in the king's household. Bathsheba remembered that when the king took her as his wife he had promised her that Solomon would ascend to the throne when he died. She saw that this was not happening and knew her own life would be in danger if Adonijah became king. Therefore, she went in to see the king and, in a very dramatic way, reminded him of his commitment to her and her son. She told the king how the elder son was claiming the throne even before the king had died.[2]

The king's response is recorded in 1 Kings 1:28–31:

> Then King David answered and said, "Call Bathsheba to me." And she came into the king's presence and stood before the king. And the king vowed and said, "As the LORD lives, who has redeemed my life from all distress, surely as I

vowed to you by the LORD, the God of Israel, saying, 'Your son Solomon shall be king after me, and he shall sit on my throne in my place'; I will indeed do so this day." Then Bathsheba bowed with her face to the ground, and prostrated herself before the king and said, "May my lord King David live forever."

It was now established! Solomon would become king!

Adonijah solved the matter. He had tried to take the kingdom by political maneuvering, but had no real love for it or any wish to fight. Therefore, fearful for his own life, he ran into the temple and begged protection from his enthroned brother. In those days a person considered ambitious for the throne would be killed immediately. Solomon had mercy on Adonijah. He spared his life, with a stern warning that any attempt to usurp the throne or cause political trouble would result in immediate death.[3]

This account is found in 1 Kings 1:50–53:

And Adonijah was afraid of Solomon, and he arose, went and took hold of the horns of the altar. Now it was told Solomon, saying, "Behold, Adonijah is afraid of King Solomon, for behold, he has taken hold of the horns of the altar, saying, 'Let King Solomon swear to me today that he will not put his servant to death with the sword.' " And Solomon said, "If he will be a worthy man, not one of his hairs will fall to the ground; but if wickedness is found in him, he will die." So King Solomon sent, and they brought him down from the altar. And he came and prostrated himself before King

Solomon, and Solomon said to him, "Go to your house."

Adonijah backed off.

During the first years of Solomon's kingship he courted Abishag, won her heart, and married her. She most likely was his first wife or at least his only true love. The "Song" was written as a reflection of their courtship. Solomon became king in the year 970 B.C. The "Song" was written five years later in 965 B.C. In our time line, it would appear that Solomon married Abishag within the first five years of his kingship.

Though Adonijah was given a strict command to be a "worthy man," in order to escape death, it seems that with time he forgot this command. He devised a plan that if successful could grant him the kingdom, but if unsuccessful could cost him his life.

We read of this plan in 1 Kings 2:13–17:

> Now Adonijah the son of Haggith came to Bathsheba the mother of Solomon. And she said, "Do you come peacefully?" And he said, "Peacefully." Then he said, "I have something {to say} to you." And she said, "Speak." So he said, "You know that the kingdom was mine and that all Israel expected me to be king; however, the kingdom has turned about and become my brother's, for it was his from the LORD. And now I am making one request of you; do not refuse me." And she said to him, "Speak." Then he said, "Please speak to Solomon the king, for he will not refuse you, that he may give me Abishag the Shunammite as a wife."

Adonijah makes his request to Bathsheba. For whatever reasons, this sounded sensible to her. She decided to grant him his request and ask for Abishag, Solomon's wife, to become Adonijah's wife. It would seem like a strange custom for one man to give another man his wife. However, things were much different in those days than they are today. Plus, we are talking about the "rights" of a king. The king had ultimate authority. Besides being commander in chief of the army and the supreme judge of his entire kingdom, he was also the absolute master of the lives of his subjects. The king could do as he pleased. In many ways he was viewed as a sovereign. If he wanted a young woman to be his wife, he got her. No one refused the king. If he wanted to get rid of a wife, he would have had that authority also.

Often the king married for political reasons, so it may have seemed reasonable to Bathsheba for Solomon to give away Abishag. Adonijah had convinced Bathsheba that he loved Abishag. Therefore, she may have even thought it best for Abishag. She obviously did not understand her son's deep affections for his wife. She agreed to make the request of her son. We read of this in 1 Kings 2:20–21:

> Then she said, "I am making one small request of you; do not refuse me." And the king said to her, "Ask, my mother, for I will not refuse you." So she said, "Let Abishag the Shunammite be given to Adonijah your brother as a wife."

Solomon erupted into a rage! This request was the straw that broke the camel's back. Adonijah was living in danger as it was. Solomon knew he wanted to be king. He knew Adonijah had tried to usurp him once before. He also knew exactly what Adonijah was up to in trying to gain the queen. Had Adonijah been given the queen he would have most likely gained the popularity of the people. This would have been a major step in eventually ousting the king. Listen to Solomon's reaction in 1 Kings 2:22:

King Solomon answered and said to his mother,
"And why are you asking Abishag the Shunammite
for Adonijah? Ask for him also the kingdom.

Not only did Solomon love Abishag, but to give her
up was to give up his kingdom.

Some have asked, "How can we be sure that the bride
in the 'Song' is Abishag?" I do not believe we can be exactly sure. However, there are some strong indications in
the Scripture that she is. Abishag is the one chosen to be
King David's nurse (see 1 Kings 1:3). Solomon obviously
falls in love with her during this time because he eventually marries her. We know this to be true because Adonijah
tried to get Solomon to give her up as his wife so she could
become his wife (see 1 Kings 2:17). Most theologians agree
that the "Song" was written about Solomon's one true love.
Since Abishag was his first wife, she seems to qualify as
the one the "Song" was written about even though
Solomon eventually had many other wives.

When Adonijah asked for the hand of Abishag,
Solomon responds in an interesting way. He says in essence, *"To ask for Abishag is the same as asking for the
kingdom."* This would not have been true unless she was
his queen. If she were merely a concubine it would not
have meant the surrender of his kingdom to give her away.

Here also, we see two types. Solomon is a type of Christ,
while Adonijah is a type of Satan. Both of them battle for
the same Bride. If Jesus were to give His Bride (the Church)
over to Satan, He would be giving over His kingdom.

THE KINGDOM OF GOD

In Luke 17:21 Jesus talks about the kingdom of God:

"Nor will they say, 'Look, here {it is!}' or,
'There {it is!}' For behold, the kingdom of God
is in your midst."

Jesus was trying to explain to His disciples that the kingdom of God was spiritual and that it was going to dwell within the heart of His bride. Satan understands this very well and subsequently wants to dwell within the heart of the would-be-Bride so that God's kingdom has no place to dwell.

Solomon had taken all he could. Adonijah had crossed the line. Solomon knew that the secret intent of his heart was to use the bride to take over the kingdom. According to the custom of the day, claiming a king's wife or concubine amounted to the same thing as claiming his throne. In a fit of rage he proclaims his own stepbrother's death. In 1 Kings 2:23–24 we read:

> Then King Solomon swore by the LORD, saying, "May God do so to me and more also, if Adonijah has not spoken this word against his own life. Now therefore, as the LORD lives, who has established me and set me on the throne of David my father, and who has made me a house as He promised, surely Adonijah will be put to death today."

This seems like bizarre behavior until we understand what is at stake. This is a battle of kingdoms. Once Satan's plan was fully exposed Jesus did the only thing he could.

> Since the children share in flesh and blood, He Himself likewise also partook of the same, that through death He might render powerless him who had the power of death, that is, the devil (Heb. 2:14).

Jesus had to "render powerless" the one who had the power of death. Other translations use the word "destroy." In either case, Jesus came to destroy, through His own death, the one who is trying to gain the affections of His Bride.

A DEFEATED FOE

Though it is important to understand Adonijah's original intentions, it is even more important to understand that once he was dealt with, he became a non-issue. Jesus stripped Satan of his power once His work on the cross was completed. Paul tells us in Ephesians that we should put on the whole armor of God so that we can stand against the "wiles" of Satan. The word "wiles" is the Greek word *methodiah*. "*Methodiah*" is the origin of the English word "method." Paul does not warn us to be prepared against the power of Satan but his methods. Satan is known as the "Father of Lies." All he can do is scheme and lie. He has no power over Christ. As we shall see in the "Song" itself, the bride's struggle was not against some outside force. Her primary struggle was with her own flesh.

Adonijah is never mentioned again in the Bible. However, this one incident is quite significant. It sets the stage for the entire love story found in the "Song."

THE COMING KING

This brings us to the other major character in this unfolding love story. Most theologians agree that Solomon himself wrote the "Song." Solomon is the king. This book depicts the great price he paid to gain the heart of his queen.

After the death of his father, Solomon becomes king. As king he can get anything he wants. No one could refuse the king. The king could have any woman as his wife. By the end of his life he had 700 wives and 300 concubines (see 1 Kings 11:3). However, things were different with Abishag. He wanted to win her heart. Most of his other wives were simply political arrangements. Abishag he loved. He did not want to simply give the command for her to be his wife, though he could have. He wanted her heart.

Solomon apparently fell in love with Abishag while

she served King David. However, he had to admire her from a distance. She was his father's nurse. Abishag was chosen for her position because of her beauty. This would be a natural draw for any young man. Solomon would have been closer to her age than King David was. However, it would have meant certain death if Solomon had tried to win her heart while she was in the king's court. Any such attempts were viewed as an attempt to dethrone the king.

For the first few years of Solomon's reign, he focused on the immediate business of the kingdom. There was much to put in order. King David had been on his bed for the last few years of his reign. Many things needed prompt attention. Once the dust settled, Solomon's affection turned again to Abishag.

The king needed a plan. Remember, Solomon was the wisest man to ever live. It's not that he was without ideas, it's just that this plan had to be perfect. The love of his life was at stake. The "Song" is the revelation of this plan. Interestingly enough, Solomon's plan to win his bride, Abishag, parallels with the King of kings' plan to win His Bride, the Church.

THE PLAN

The "Song" reveals to us that Solomon disguised himself as a shepherd and began to tend his sheep next to Abishag's vineyard. Initially, Abishag failed to realize who it was who was attempting to win her heart. This is evident by her comments in the opening chapter of the "Song." She identifies him as a shepherd, grazing his flocks in Song 1:7:

> "Tell me, O you whom my soul loves, Where do you pasture [your flock,] Where do you make [it] lie down at noon? For why should I be like one who veils herself Beside the flocks of your companions?"

Some may ask the question, "How is it she did not recognize him as the king?"

First of all, Solomon had to admire Abishag from a distance while she served his father, King David. Secondly, she considered herself a failure, unworthy of such attention by the king. It is not difficult for me to see how this could happen. I lived the first 21 years of my life before I recognized that the one trying to win my heart was actually the Son of God.

Solomon is a type of Christ. Abishag is a type of the Church or the bride of Christ (see Appendix). Christ our King came to earth clothed as a man to win the heart of His Bride and to prepare her for His ultimate return. At first we did not recognize Him for who He really was. As King of kings and Lord of lords, He could have rightly demanded our betrothal, but He wanted to win our hearts. So the King of kings disguised himself as one of us, to eventually win us and convert us.

Abishag ultimately fell in love with this mysterious shepherd who had shown her an unusual amount of attention. Whenever she was around him she felt protected, loved, and provided for. This was a wonderful change for her since she was rejected by her own family and friends. Though she felt completely unworthy of his attention, she loved every minute of it.

The proposal that Solomon disguised himself as a shepherd is pure conjecture. However, the "Song's" New Testament parallel, the gospel, allows us to see some things about Solomon that may not be written. Though the "Song" itself is a "looking back" at the courtship of Solomon and Abishag, to fully understand it we must do a "looking back" ourselves from a different perspective. This goes back to the "law of mutual resemblance" defined in the introduction of this book. This "law" states that Scripture interprets Scripture. In other words, the most effective way to gain insight into this Old Testament portion of Scripture, which reveals what Solomon did to win the heart of his bride, is to consider the New Testament portion of Scripture which reveals what Jesus did to win the heart of His bride: He became one of us. We must first understand the gospel in order to properly understand the "Song."

CHAPTER TWO

ARISE, MY DARLING!

"My beloved responded and said to me, 'Arise, my darling, my beautiful one, and come along' " (Song of Sol. 2:10).

These are the words of the groom wooing his love. We begin to see here the process of abandonment that the bride must go through to prepare herself for all that the king has for her. Solomon wants to reveal himself to her, but she must first arise and ascend to the place of revelation. He has a secret place high up on Mount Hermon where this revelation will occur.

The call to "arise" was the bride's introduction to the crucified life. He challenges her a second time in verse 13:

" 'The fig tree has ripened its figs, And the vines in blossom have given forth {their} fragrance. Arise, my darling, my beautiful one, And come along!' "

The Bible has one paradox after another in it. Solomon asking his bride to "arise" in order to "go down" is a paradox. By "going down" I mean that of "dying to self."

INCREDIBLE!

The crucified life is a paradox at best. We must go down to go up. I found an old article in my files that I believe we need to consider. It describes some of what the crucified life means.

If you are a Christian, you believe some incredible things! You believe that you were once a walking dead man while you were still alive. You believe that though still alive, you are really dead, and while already dead, you are more alive than ever before. Though you fully expect to die, when you do, you will be alive forever. Incredible!

You believe that, though already dead, you were one day slain on a cross. Yet, the very cross that slew you gave you priceless life. Though you were crucified on the cross, you actually were not, because a sinless substitute, the Lord Jesus Christ, was there in your stead. Consequently, when you see a Cross it means death, and you glory in it, because it has given you life. You remain on earth to die, so you can go to heaven to live, yet if you do not "die" before death, you cannot live after death. Though you are in the world, you do everything opposite to its general pattern. You hate the world so you can win the world. You tell people they are condemned and lost so that they might be saved. Incredible!

If you have a family you give them to the Lord, not because you do not want to keep them but because you do! If you have possessions you plead not to own them, not to disown them but to be entrusted with them in a much greater way. Anything you keep you know you will lose! Anything you lose, you know you will find again!

That you might save your life, you lay it down! You go down in prayer that you might rise in devotion! If you refuse to go down in humbleness you are already down. When you start down, you are really on your way up. When you feel strong you are weak! When you are weakest the Bible says you are then strong! You may have an abounding table, yet if you cover a morsel it will turn bitter. You may be destitute and poor but you can make others wealthy with a word. When you possess riches you lose the power to enrich others! You have the most after you have given the most away! That is incredible!

To be forgiven once, you can forgive seventy times seven. You will go two miles when asked to go one. If a man wants your shirt, you will offer him your coat also. You will be defrauded by a brother, not because he is your brother, but because you want to be a brother to him.

Yes it's true! If you are a Christian, you believe some incredible things! (anonymous)

THE PLACE OF PRAYER

Abishag's problem was that she was self-centered. This caused many problems in relationship to the crucified life. Initially she based her love on what she could gain from him, which is a self-love.

Solomon has a wonderful revelation for her, but he could not disclose it to her in her carnal condition. He called her to follow him to the secret place, but in order for her to follow him, she must die to self. She cannot "see" who he really is until she loves him more than she loves herself.

" 'Arise, my darling, my beautiful one, And come along!'

"O my dove, in the clefts of the rock, In the secret place of the steep pathway, Let me see your form, Let me hear your voice; For your voice is sweet, And your form is lovely" (Song of Sol. 2:13–14).

This is the call to the secret place, the place of prayer. We must arise to the place of prayer. The problem with the prayer life is that it has some very steep steps leading up to it. However, it is in the place of prayer where we hear His voice and He hears our voice. We behold Him and He beholds us. This is what makes the steep ascent worth it all.

The whole struggle of abandonment is the challenge of the steep pathway. The crucified life causes us to ascend spiritually. However, there are challenges on the path upward. This complicates the whole issue. All the large animals lived in the high country. There were mountain lions and leopards in the high country. Solomon talks of them in chapter 4.

"{Come} with me from Lebanon, {my} bride, May you come with me from Lebanon. Journey down from the summit of Amana, From the summit of Senir and Hermon, From the dens of lions, From the mountains of leopards" (Song of Sol. 4:8).

The challenge of the crucified life is faith. There are lions and leopards that want to challenge the path we are on. It takes faith to die to self. It takes faith to believe that Jesus will care for us. When my wife and I started Pray-Tell Ministries, we felt God telling us to travel without health insurance. That was a lion attempting to scare me away from the development of this ministry. We slowly followed God upward, but to do that, we had to die to self and the belief that we had to care for ourselves. Eventually we defeated that lion, but it was not an easy struggle. Today I would not think of putting my trust in health insurance. The need for health insurance is now a dead lion.

We have to understand that this is not a call to walk the path alone. We are ascending with the Lord. Jesus is found in selflessness. He is nowhere to be found in selfishness. If we want to walk with Him, we must die to self.

Consider what Solomon learned from this process of bringing his bride-to-be out of a slothful, self-centered lifestyle into one of abandonment or selflessness. He shares some of his wisdom with us in Proverbs 26:13: "The sluggard says, 'There is a lion in the road! A lion is in the open square!' "

The self-centered man does not want to face the battles of abandonment. They seem too overwhelming to him. The very thought of a lion is reason enough for him to stay right where he is.

LION DEFEATERS

Then Samson went down to Timnah with his father and mother . . . and behold, a young lion {came} roaring toward him. And the Spirit of the LORD came upon him mightily, so that he tore him as one tears a kid (Judg. 14:5–6).

But David said to Saul, "Your servant was tending his father's sheep. When a lion or a bear came and took a lamb from the flock . . . I seized {him} by his beard and struck him and killed him (1 Sam. 17:34–35).

Then Benaiah the son of Jehoiada, the son of a valiant man. . . . went down and killed a lion in the middle of a pit on a snowy day (2 Sam. 23:20).

Samson, David, and Benaiah each killed a lion with their bare hands. Did they do it alone? No! God was with them. In Samson's case it says that the Spirit of the Lord came upon him mightily. If only we could understand that when we follow God to the crucified life, we walk with Him. When the lion attacks us, God is beside us, strengthening us. What could we not handle while walking hand-in-hand with our Lord?

DANIEL

Consider Daniel's life. Daniel had a testimony of being a person who sought God. He lived the crucified life. Because of his favor with God, Daniel was growing in influence. He became one of three commissioners, appointed to watch over 120 satraps.

> And over them three commissioners (of whom Daniel was one), that these satraps might be accountable to them, and that the king might not suffer loss (Dan. 6:2).

His influence was making those around him jealous, so they decided to snare Daniel by designing an injunction making it illegal to pray to any god. They convinced the king to sign the injunction. Yet, when Daniel learned of the injunction, it did not keep him from praying. He knew that it would endanger his life to pray to his God, but he continued.

> Now when Daniel knew that the document was signed, he entered his house (now in his roof chamber he had windows open toward Jerusalem); and he continued kneeling on his knees three times a day, praying and giving thanks before his God, as he had been doing previously (Dan. 6:10).

Daniel's perspective of faith was different from that which is common today. He did not see faith as something that would keep him from all harm.

The satraps caught Daniel praying: "Then these men came by agreement and found Daniel making petition and supplication before his God" (Dan. 6:11).

Because of this, the king was forced to put Daniel in the lions' den.

> Then the king gave orders, and Daniel was brought in and cast into the lions' den. The king spoke and said to Daniel, "Your God whom you constantly serve will Himself deliver you" (Dan. 6:16).

Daniel's God did deliver him! I find it very interesting that Daniel went into the lions' den as a direct result of prayer. His persecution came because of the fact that he sought God. Daniel's pursuit of God did not assure him a comfortable life. It brought lions onto his path. However, it was also because of prayer that Daniel could walk out of the lions' den. Is it not much better to be able to face the lions and defeat them than to live in fear of encountering them?

I MUST ARISE

> "I must arise now and go about the city; In the streets and in the squares I must seek him whom my soul loves" (Song of Sol. 3:2).

Solomon was continually trying to bring Abishag into maturity. He wanted to reveal many things to her that he could not reveal until she was willing to come to the secret place. With time she began to mature. In this verse, we see her now seeking him on her own. She said, "I must arise." Before this, Solomon perpetually encouraged her to arise, now she displays her maturity when she says, "I must arise."

Before coming into the secret place, she based her prayer life on her own needs. She was forced to pray because of the lions. These lions (challenges) were the basis of her prayer life. Because of her self-focus, she was still praying primarily to get her own needs met. But then she changed. She came into a pursuit of Him. She initiates the pursuit. Her desire for intimacy with Him defeated the lions.

It is a sign great of spiritual maturity to seek God on your own. It used to be the groom saying, "Please arise, please come into the secret place." Now it's the bride saying, "I must arise. I must go to the place of prayer."

"I must seek him whom my soul loves."

Those who develop a pursuit of Him find that the lions no longer mean what they once did. Once they were the basis of their entire prayer life. Now they hardly even give them any thought. Now their prayer life is based on their desire to be with Him. When they enter the secret place, they do so to hear His voice. They want Him to hear their voice also, not their plea, just their voice. They want Him to hear of the love they have just for Him. They want Him to see their form (heart). They also want to see His form. Now they want Him, the one whom their soul loves, not just things from Him.

LOOK AT HIM!

"Go forth, O daughters of Zion, And gaze on King Solomon with the crown With which his mother has crowned him On the day of his wedding, And on the day of his gladness of heart" (Song of Sol. 3:11).

When we are immature, we want people to look at us, so we can be admired. We want others to talk of our greatness. However, as we grow spiritually our attention shifts from us to Him. In this verse we find Abishag talking about the wedding day. She refers to their wedding day as the "day of his gladness of heart." More important than that, she is not seeking any attention for herself. She charges the daughters of Zion to gaze upon the king.

It is interesting to think that this is the bride dressed up in her wedding gown saying in essence, "Do not look at me, look at him!" This addresses the transformation that takes place in the secret place. The thing that keeps us from the secret place is our love of self. Once our love of self diminishes and our love of Him increases we can enter into intimacy with Him.

In the secret place we see Him. Once seen, there is nothing more beautiful. Once seen, we are obsessed with showing Him to others. Once seen, the desire for self-exaltation dies, we are now taken up with His exaltation. That is to be the way of our life.

Keep in mind, the "Song" was written in an oriental fashion. The scenes do not fall in the kind of sequence we may be used to. In chapter 2 we see Solomon wooing Abishag, challenging her to give up her love of self. In chapter three we see Abishag talking about what happened in her life after she ascended to the secret place. However, we do not have a picture of her ascending to the secret place until the fourth chapter. Therefore, chapter 3 is a "looking back" by the bride at what happened because of her going to the secret place.

THE SECRET PLACE

"{Come} with me from Lebanon, {my} bride, May you come with me from Lebanon. Journey down from the summit of Amana, From the summit of Senir and Hermon" (Song of Sol. 4:8).

Solomon apparently succeeded in bringing Abishag to Mount Hermon where his secret place is. In chapter 4 we see them descending from the summit of the mount. It is possible that Mount Hermon held a special place in the heart of Solomon. Mount Hermon, known as the "sacred mountain," may have been a place King David brought the child Solomon to. The mountain formed the northernmost boundary of the country beyond the Jordan which Israel took from the Amorites. Its height is 9,101 feet above the Mediterranean Sea. It is by far the highest of all mountains in or near Palestine. Hermon was the religious center of primeval Syria.

The view from the snow-clad Mount Hermon is magnificent. From the Dead Sea region, its snows can be seen 120 miles away. Its melting snows form the main source of the Jordan and the rivers that water the Damascus plateau.

King David speaks of the "dew of Hermon," (see Ps. 133:3). Apparently the king frequented the mount to gain a perspective of his kingdom that he could not gain from any other place. Is it possible that Solomon, the boy, went with his father from time to time to the top of the mountain? It would be very typical of a young boy to go exploring on the mountain.

I grew up in the Black Hills of South Dakota. The highest point in the Black Hills is Harney Peak. It rises over 7,200 feet above sea level. It, too, is snow-capped much of the year. When I was a young boy my family would go camping in the hills quite regularly. We would walk the different paths, climb rocky cliffs, and go fishing.

It would not surprise me at all to find that the boy Solomon adventured along a deer path with his dad. He may have climbed a rocky cliff himself as King David ascended to the top of the mount. It's possible that on one of those adventures Solomon discovered a "secret place." It could have been a place where he was protected. It could have been a place far from the vision of anyone. It could have become his special hiding place. Regardless of the authenticity of that, we do see in the "Song" that King Solomon wanted to bring Abishag to the top of the mount. He wanted to bring her to his "secret place" so he could reveal to her something no one else knew.

FROM OBSCURITY TO ROYALTY

In the first seven verses of the fourth chapter of the "Song," Solomon openly declared his love for Abishag.

> "How beautiful you are, my darling, How beautiful you are! Your eyes are {like} doves behind your veil; Your hair is like a flock of goats That have descended from Mount Gilead" (Song of Sol. 4:1).

After she paid the price of ascension, Solomon was ready to hold nothing back. She needed to understand who this "shepherd" really was. He needed to propose marriage. Guynes says:

> Solomon knew what he must do. She must know who he really is, and the manner in which he revealed himself was very important. Finally, they reached the summit. It was a breathtaking view.
>
> Solomon may have said, "Look on the west side. You can see all the way to the Great Sea (Mediterranean Sea), and then look eastward all the way to the great deserts of Arabia. If you look to the north, you can see all the way to Syria and looking southward you can see far beyond Jerusalem.
>
> "Do you know who owns all of this?" he may have asked.
>
> "Of course," she perhaps replied. "It belongs to Solomon, the most powerful king in all the world," and she may have thought, *I knew him when he was just a young boy in his father's palace.* But of course her shepherd-friend wouldn't understand, so she wouldn't say something like that. And maybe it was just when that memory was flashing through her mind that things began to fall into place.[1]

Solomon decided it was time. For this occasion he wore his royal robes under his shepherd's garb. After his great confession of love for Abishag, he began to discard his shepherd's clothing. He removed his head covering, then his outer garment. Underneath were the royal robes of the king himself. Abishag could not believe what she saw.

My shepherd is the king! she thought to herself.

How can this be? she reels, *I failed his father. I was sent back to my home. I did not measure up.*

Solomon then revealed to her that he had come to take her from obscurity to royalty and that he wanted to give to her everything she saw. He asked her to marry him. Can you imagine this love scene? Here we have the most powerful king in the world telling an obscure field worker that she will become his queen. Is that not what our King Jesus has done for each of us? Has He not brought us out of obscurity to royalty? Has He not given us the keys to His kingdom?

She accepted his proposal. This is why he called her "his bride" when he invited her to descend from Mount Hermon. Now that Solomon has won her heart his attention focuses on preparing her for the wedding day.

TRANSFIGURED/TRANSFORMED

It's quite interesting that Solomon's secret place, or place of revelation, was on Mount Hermon. Most theologians today believe that the Mount Hermon region was the scene of our Lord's transfiguration. If so, Christ traveled from Bethsaida, on the northwest shore of the Sea of Galilee, to the coasts of Caesarea Philippi; from there He led His disciples to a high mountain.

> Six days later Jesus took with Him Peter and James and John his brother, and brought them up to a high mountain by themselves. And He was transfigured before them; and His face shone like the sun, and His garments became as white as light (Matt. 17:1–2).

Peter, James, and John were willing to pay the price of separation and ascend with the Lord to the top of Mount Hermon. It was there that Jesus was transfigured before them and they were transformed.

They could not believe what they were seeing. They must have thought, *Truly this is the Son of God! Could it also be true that He has come to offer us a position in His Kingdom?* Much to their pleasure they found out it is all true! The King of kings had come to bring us from obscurity to royalty.

Peter answered and said to Jesus, "Lord, it is good for us to be here; if You wish, I will make three tabernacles here, one for You, and one for Moses, and one for Elijah" (Matt. 17:4).

Peter was so excited that he could not stop talking. Here we have a big hunk of a man, a fisherman by trade, talking incessantly like an excited bride-to-be. The first thing he talked about was building a house. Is it not typical of a bride to be interested in a house? But they could not stay there. They had to come down the mountain. They had to descend, much like Solomon and Abishag had to descend. The disciples could not stay on the mountaintop because there was much to do in the Kingdom.

As they were coming down from the mountain, Jesus commanded them, saying, "Tell the vision to no one until the Son of Man has risen from the dead" (Matt. 17:9).

MY BRIDE MY KINGDOM

"Your teeth are like a flock of {newly} shorn ewes Which have come up from {their} washing, All of which bear twins, And not one among them has lost her young. Your lips are like a scarlet thread, And your mouth is lovely. Your temples are like a slice of a pomegranate Behind your veil. Your neck is like the tower of David Built with rows of stones, On which are hung a thousand shields, All the round shields of the mighty men" (Song of Sol. 4:2–4).

Solomon took advantage of Abishag's ability to see the greatness of his kingdom (from the top of Mount Hermon) to cause her to see something even greater. He revealed to her that she in essence was his true kingdom. That which she viewed with her eyes was mere dirt, stone, and grass. What glory was there in being king over the dirt? Solomon was glorying in that of reigning in the heart of his bride.

He used all the things that would mean much to any earthly ruler (a flock of ewes, a scarlet thread, a tower of mighty men) and attributed these qualities to his bride. He was trying to tell her that she meant everything to him. She was in essence, his kingdom (see Conclusion).

REVELATION REQUIRES SEPARATION

Isn't it interesting how people want great power and revelation without any kind of voluntary separation in their lives? The key to revelation is separation. However, it's not just separation, it's *voluntary separation*. Many Christians have been called apart from the main flow of the world, and yet have no sense of spirituality because they lack a voluntary separation. They really have no pursuit of the Lord. Their prayer life is based upon their need, not their desire. Those who gain revelation, *willfully* pray. They separate themselves through their desire to be with the Lord.

At first, Solomon was wooing his bride to arise. However, she never did really come into any understanding of who he was until she began to cause herself to arise. Once she said, "I must arise," she was brought to the secret place. Once she brought herself to the place of pursuing him, she came into great revelation.

This really is a very simple principle. God is spirit, and we are flesh and blood. We live in a carnal world. He lives in a spirit world. If we are going to gain insight into

His realm, we must separate ourselves from our current existence. What I mean by separation is simply this: We must willfully abstain from some "lawful," worldly activities. There are many things we could do as Christians, but should not do. If we want to maintain any sense of holiness about us there must be willful separation.

When I have coffee with other ministers, and they talk about going to the latest Hollywood movies, I feel separated from them. The Lord simply speaks to me and says, "That is not to be a part of your existence." That is a "voluntary separation" my wife and I have decided to live by. Subsequently, I do not know much about what is happening in the "movie world." However, when others talk to me about it, I am made more aware of the presence of God that is in my life. That presence comes from my voluntary separation.

When we practice the presence of the world we cannot expect to live in the presence of the Lord. It seems that few men willfully and purposefully spend time in prayer, and yet they expect a power when they do pray that simply cannot be there. They try to "work up" power through faith and loud praying rather than allowing power to come through separation. Have you ever heard of power without holiness? The word "holiness" simply means, "separation." To live "holy," one must live in willful separation.

THE LITTLE FOXES

"Catch the foxes for us, The little foxes that are ruining the vineyards, While our vineyards are in blossom" (Song of Sol. 2:15).

Immediately after bringing Abishag to the secret place, the place of revelation, Solomon begins to talk to her about the vineyard. The vineyard represents the work of God. God calls us to the secret place of prayer so we can gain revelation about His work. He says, "Catch the foxes for us." The little foxes are those things that are bringing the vineyard or "the work of God" to ruin.

God wants to bring us to the place of prayer so He can give us insight into His work. Coming into the place of prayer is that of joining Him in His work. Not until we separate ourselves from our world and enter His world can we hear His voice. In the secret place we hear His voice, and He hears our voice. But if we do not enter in, we really do not involve ourselves in His work.

Oswald Chambers once said, "Prayer is not what we do so that we can enter into the greater work, prayer is the greater work."

How can we expect to be effective in the work of God if we lack the needed closeness to Him that allows us to hear His voice? To be effective in His work, we must know what He is saying. We must walk worthy of our calling. We must hear Him.

BLOW UPON MY GARDEN

"How beautiful is your love, my sister, {my} bride! How much better is your love than wine, And the fragrance of your oils Than all {kinds} of spices! . . . Awake, O north {wind,} And come, {wind of} the south; Make my garden breathe out {fragrance,} Let its spices be wafted abroad. May my beloved come into his garden And eat its choice fruits!" (Song of Sol. 4:10–16).

Solomon had his bride-to-be on the top of Mount Hermon and wanted the whole world to know of her beauty. He spoke of her love as better than wine and that she now possessed the oil and fragrances that bring pleasure to him. The ointments and perfumes that issued from her, the gifts and graces of the Spirit and her good works, are an odor of a sweet smell, a sacrifice acceptable, well-pleasing to God (see Phil. 4:18).

Solomon wanted the whole world to know of his bride. He called for the winds to blow upon her on the mountaintop to spread her fragrance throughout the land.

As we grow in the things of God, we develop within us the very qualities and attributes that initially drew us to Christ. In other words, those things that attracted us to Christ have now become a part of us. God now uses those things to attract others to himself.

Christ has now ascended to heaven, and we are left as a bride-in-waiting. However, we have been given an assignment. We are to continue to pursue Him. We are to develop in His character. We are to be a revelation of Him to a lost world. As the world looks upon us, they are to see our dedication to Him. They are to smell the sweet fragrance of our lives and be drawn to Him in the same way we were.

REDEMPTION'S SONG

Consider carefully the following Scripture verses:

"As for your birth, on the day you were born your navel cord was not cut, nor were you washed with water for cleansing; you were not rubbed with salt or even wrapped in cloths. No eye looked with pity on you to do any of these things for you, to have compassion on you. Rather you were thrown out into the open field, for you were abhorred on the day you were born.

"When I passed by you and saw you squirming in your blood, I said to you {while you were} in your blood, 'Live!' I said to you while you were in your blood, 'Live!' I made you numerous like plants of the field. Then you grew up, became tall, and reached the age for fine ornaments; {your} breasts were formed and your hair had grown. Yet you were naked and bare. Then I passed by you and saw you, and behold, you were at the time for love; so I spread My skirt over you and covered your nakedness. I also swore to you and entered into a covenant with you so that you became Mine," declares the Lord GOD. "Then I bathed you with water, washed off your blood from you, and anointed you with oil. I also clothed you with embroidered cloth, and put sandals of porpoise skin on your feet; and I wrapped you with fine linen and covered you with silk. And I adorned you with ornaments, put bracelets on your hands, and a necklace around your neck. I also put a ring in your nostril, earrings in your ears, and a beautiful crown on your head. Thus you were adorned with gold and silver, and your dress was of fine linen, silk, and embroidered cloth. You ate fine flour, honey, and oil; so you were exceedingly beautiful and advanced to royalty. Then your fame went forth among the nations on account of your beauty, for it was perfect because of My splendor which I bestowed on you," declares the Lord GOD (Ezek. 16:4–14).

Though the preceding verses come from the Book of Ezekiel they capsulize the essence of Solomon's wonderful message. The "Song of Songs" is THE song of all songs. It is our song of redemption. This is the song we will sing throughout all eternity. It is the song of how our King of kings came to earth as mere man to redeem us from our sin. It's about how He covered our sinfulness and cleansed us. It is the song of Him bringing us from obscurity to royalty. The "Song of Solomon" is the account of our own betrothal to our Lord, the King of all kings. As Dr. Guynes once said, "This book is the great Old Testament parable of the grace of God that was to come."

CHAPTER FOUR

DRAW ME

"Draw me after you {and} let us run {together!} The king has brought me into his chambers. We will rejoice in you and be glad; We will extol your love more than wine. Rightly do they love you" (Song of Sol. 1:4).

I n this simple prayer of, "Draw me after you," the bride is expressing her desire to be brought near to her love. This is possibly the most powerful prayer in the Bible. "Draw me" is a disclosure of the weakness of our flesh and yet an expression of desire. Typically, our flesh does not crave spiritual things. Jesus explains this to us in John 6:44: "No one can come to Me unless the Father who sent Me draws him."

We must be drawn to our love by Him. Our flesh fights this drawing every step of the way. The Spirit and the flesh are at odds within us. Jesus told Peter this when he (Peter) was struggling with prayer. Jesus had entered the Garden to pray and wanted His disciples to join him but finds them sleeping.

And He came to the disciples and found them sleeping, and said to Peter, "So, you {men}

could not keep watch with Me for one hour?
Keep watching and praying, that you may not
enter into temptation; the spirit is willing, but
the flesh is weak (Matt. 26:40–41).

The Spirit of God within us cries out for spiritual
things. When we hear things that pertain to drawing close
to God, the Spirit of God within says, "Yes, that is what I
need." Shortly after that our flesh says, "You cannot do
those things, you cannot develop a prayer life, you do not
have the time it would take, you are much too busy." This
is also expressed in Galatians 5:17:

For the flesh sets its desire against the Spirit,
and the Spirit against the flesh; for these are in
opposition to one another, so that you may not
do the things that you please.

When the bride prays, "Draw me," she is expressing
her desire to overcome her flesh. This prayer also implies
a sense of distance from Him, and a desire for union with
Him. "Draw me, else I move not," is the essence of her
prayer. We are not driven to Christ, but drawn in such a
way as is agreeable to us as rational creatures. We would
most likely rebel against being driven to God but find being drawn quite fitting.

The flowing forth of the soul after Christ, and its
ready compliance with Him, are the effects of His grace;
we could not run after Him if He did not draw us. Paul
the apostle teaches us this very thing.

Not that we are adequate in ourselves to
consider anything as {coming} from ourselves,
but our adequacy is from God, who also made
us adequate {as} servants of a new covenant, not
of the letter, but of the Spirit; for the letter kills,
but the Spirit gives life (2 Cor. 3:5–6).

The "Song" reveals the process of abandonment the bride is going through. She must abandon self and learn to love Him more than she loves herself. The only way for this to be possible is for her to recognize that it is going to take a power greater than what she now possesses. This simple prayer of, "Draw me," is a very similar prayer to the one we prayed when we asked Christ to come into our lives.

When we made Christ our Savior by asking Him to forgive our sins, we put ourselves into the process of dying to self. The whole Christian life is defined by the term, "dying to self." For many years I traveled to Hawaii two to three times a year to teach a class for Youth With A Mission (YWAM). The class was a part of their "Discipleship Training School." The initials for the school are "D.T.S." The students that were going through the class did not call the class by its official name. They said "D.T.S." stood for "Dying To Self."

Dying to self is really the essence of Christian discipleship. If it were easy to "die," we would not struggle with it so much. Dying to self could also be called the process of developing faith. The Church in America has completely reversed the purpose of faith. We are teaching people that we should use faith to gain, while the Bible teaches that faith is what we need to die. It takes faith to die.

The faith of Jesus was displayed in His death. Jesus showed us the proper use of faith when He went to the grave with a complete confidence that His Father would raise Him from the dead. In the "Song," the groom is trying to get the bride to give up her life and to surrender it to him. Her struggle is that of believing that he can actually raise her up if she does die.

When we are asked to have faith, we are in essence being asked to die. We are asked to die to the situation we are faced with and let God bring life to it. When we bring things to God in prayer, we are in essence expressing our inability to handle our lives. We actually are turning it over to Him, or dying to self. When we give our tithes and offerings, we are dying to our means of caring for ourselves financially. In each case we are laying our lives down, believing that God will bring life to us through it. Faith results in gaining, but its use is for giving.

EVANGELISM

When Christ, by His Spirit, draws us, we must, with our spirits, run after Him. As God says, "I will, and you shall" (see Ezek. 36:27), so we must say, "You shall and we will; you shall work in us both to will and to do, and therefore we will work out our own salvation" (see Phil. 2:12–13). Running after Him denotes eagerness of desire, readiness of affection, vigor of pursuit, and swiftness of motion.

When the bride says, "Draw me, and we will run after thee," she is saying in essence, "Not only will I follow you as fast as I can, but I will bring all mine along with me: I and the virgins that love thee (see Song of Sol. 1:3–4).

Intimacy is the impetus for evangelism. She wants others to experience what she has experienced. She wants others to come into intimacy with Him also. It is very typical for those who love Jesus deeply to want others to love Him deeply also.

Without intimacy, evangelism can become simply religious work. Some men are motivated to evangelize. Some men are gifted in this area. However, to go about the work of God without the God of the work is not what God has called us to. The work of God is not to be empowered by our own strength but by the prompting and wooing of the Spirit of God. We are to do all things out of a craving and deep desire to bring others into intimacy with God.

ONE GROOM, MANY BRIDES!

The Church is often called the bride of Christ. However, the Church is made up of all the believers who ever were and ever will be. So although we are one Bride (capital "B") we are made up of several brides (small "b"). There is, however, only one true Husband, Jesus Christ. Jesus has only one Bride and yet many brides simultaneously. With man, this is a problem. Man is corrupt. His unregenerate heart and nature take advantage of others. But with God this is no problem at all because of true love.

What carnal man understands is lust. Lust is a false self-love. It only considers itself and its needs. Love, on the other hand, is different. Consider what the Scripture says about true love:

> Love is patient, love is kind, {and} is not jealous; love does not brag {and} is not arrogant, does not act unbecomingly; it does not seek its own, is not provoked, does not take into account a wrong {suffered,} does not rejoice in unrighteousness, but rejoices with the truth; bears all things, believes all things, hopes all things, endures all things (1 Cor. 13:4–7).

The regenerate heart understands a little (very little) about true love in how it rejoices over another person's relationship with Jesus. There is no jealousy at all. We want others to know Jesus very intimately. Our own intimacy with Christ propels us to bring others to Him. Isn't it interesting to think that we are the bride of Christ but our greatest desire is to share Him with others?

I was in a church service once when the truth of this hit me. I had just preached about intimacy with the Lord and had called people to the altar. There was a wonderful, sweet presence of God there that night. Many people wept softly as they sought the face of Christ. As I was walking back and forth among the people who were praying, my heart rejoiced at the presence of God which *they* were experiencing. As I was simply walking and praying, God spoke a simple truth to my heart. He said, *"True love wants other peoples' needs met before your own."* True love has no jealousy. True love longs for others to know Jesus intimately.

As we read the Old Testament we find that many "men of God" had several wives. Solomon had 700 wives. He also had 300 concubines. Man corrupts everything with his lust and greed. This makes it difficult to see how one man with many wives could be a "type" of things to come. Yet it is possible that one man with many wives was a type of one God with many wives.

In the Old Testament, God did not dwell within the heart of man. The presence of God was found in the Holy of Holies. The priests that entered the Holy of Holies to offer sacrifices for the people had to be completely pure. Sin in the priest's life would have been interpreted as another god in his life. They even tied a rope around the priest so they could pull him out in case God struck him dead because of sin in his life. If he did die, they could not go in and take his body out because they themselves would have died in the presence of God also, hence the rope. The presence of God demanded a very high standard of purity and loyalty.

In the New Testament, God dwells in the hearts of men. Our bodies are His temple. The Holy of Holies is within us. I believe there is a different standard for us today because of this. In the Old Testament, men often had many wives. That, however, did not seem to mean what it would mean today, because God did not dwell within the heart of men. Man was not God's temple in the Old Testament as He is today. The One who is holy and pure dwells within us today. Subsequently, we have a different standard of holiness.

Though the bride of Christ is made up of many individuals, there is only one Bride. Jesus only has one Bride! Today, husbands, who represent Christ, are to have only one wife. For a man to have more than one wife would be symbolic of Jesus having more than one love in His life. Jesus gave His life for His Bride. He loves no other.

THE CHAMBERS

When the bride prayed to be drawn, she had an immediate answer. "The King has drawn me, has brought me into his chambers." The struggle is not in coming into the chambers. The struggle is in *wanting* to be brought into the chambers. Once the bride finally came to the place of saying, "Draw me," she was drawn immediately.

The chambers is the place of intimacy; it is Solomon's secret place. The introduction to this book said that the "Song" is a "looking back" at the courtship and eventual marriage of Solomon and Abishag. The first four verses of the book are the expressions of the bride once she came into the secret place or the chambers. The verses that follow the opening scene reveal what took place to bring her to the chambers.

As she followed him up the mountain, as she ascended the steep pathway, it's possible she ran out of her own strength. She then says, "Draw me, I do not have the strength to do this on my own. However, I do want to be brought into the chambers (the secret place)." The king immediately helps her and brings her into his secret place.

It is not hard for us to relate to the bride's dilemma. I know of many times in my life when my heart was running after God. I would ache to be brought into intimacy with Him. I would work hard at my prayer life. However, often I would run into a steep cliff that I could not ascend. In those times I would simply have to say, "Jesus, help me! I cannot do this on my own. I call upon your grace."

How does one describe the secret place? I do not believe God intends for any of us to reveal the intimacies of our relationship with Him. Intimacy is the heart of any relationship. It is where one is fully exposed. It is where one is fully known. It is where one is fully protected. The secret place is a very special place that is just between the two of you. It must remain private.

> For in the day of trouble He will conceal me in His tabernacle; In the secret place of His tent He will hide me; He will lift me up on a rock (Ps. 27:5).

Though the secret place is a most wonderful place, it is only for those who seek it out. We do not simply happen to enter the secret place with the Lord. It is a place that one must strive for. Only those who follow the Lord in the hard, steep places are brought into it.

> The secret of the LORD is for those who fear Him, And He will make them know His covenant (Ps. 25:14).

Those who fear Him enter the secret place. The "Song" reveals the process of abandonment the bride is going through. She does not enter the secret place until her heart becomes absorbed with her one true love. Not until she holds him in deep reverence is she willing to climb the steep pathway. However, once she ascends to the top of the mountain she enters the secret place. Once she was willing to live the crucified life, she entered in. Once she was willing to give up her own goals, her own ambitions, and her own dreams, she entered in. Once she took on His goals, His ambitions, and His dreams, she entered in.

Many people want intimacy with the Lord without paying the price of abandonment. They want a closeness to the Lord. But they want that closeness without spending time in His presence. They want to possess God without God possessing them. It will not work! We must do what the bride did and pray, "Draw me, Lord!"

LORD, I WANT YOU

I remember the Lord taking me through a transitional time in my prayer life. When I first started giving myself to a life of prayer, I was quite typical as a pray-er. I would express my desire, my love, and my worship of Him. Often I would say repeatedly, "Lord, I want you." I would get very absorbed with that. I would spend my first hour in prayer saying, "Lord, I want you." I wanted God. I wanted to know God, not just know about God.

I now realize how this prayer of, "Lord, I want you," was not bringing myself into more intimacy with Him. One day Jesus began to deal with me about what I was praying. He caused me to see the lack of surrender on my part by simply praying for more of the Lord. This eventually changed my prayer. I went from saying, "Lord, I want you," to saying, "Lord, I want you to have me." I was wanting God without any subsequent surrender on my part. I went from seeking the Lord for myself to giving myself to the Lord.

The simple prayer of, "Lord, I want you to have me," expresses a surrender of the bride to the groom. There cannot be any intimacy without surrender. I have said for many years that the secret of the kingdom is not based on how much of God we can get. The secret of the kingdom is based on how much of us the Lord can get. The kingdom of God comes through our surrender of ourselves to Him.

CHAPTER FIVE

NO HESITATION

"I have come into my garden, my sister, {my} bride; I have gathered my myrrh along with my balsam" (Song of Sol. 5:1).

In chapter 5 of the "Song," the groom has come into his garden, which could also be called his secret place. He begins to call for his bride to join him. The groom has been working in the vineyard, which is symbolic of the work of God, and wants his bride to join him in this work. This is a very important call. It's the call to intercession. However, the bride is asleep.

"I was asleep, but my heart was awake. A voice! My beloved was knocking: 'Open to me, my sister, my darling, My dove, my perfect one! For my head is drenched with dew, My locks with the damp of the night' " (Song of Sol. 5:2).

The bride is asleep when the call to intercession comes to her. If we compare this to when Christ comes into the Garden of Gethsemane, we find an interesting similarity.

And He came to the disciples and found them sleeping, and said to Peter, "So, you {men}

could not keep watch with Me for one hour?"
(Matt. 26:40).

Jesus wants His disciples to join Him. This event is
one of the most important events in the history of mankind. The Son of God is about to go to the cross to pay
the penalty for our sins. He seeks the support of His disciples, but they are asleep. He awakens them hoping they
will join Him but they hesitate and finally fall back to sleep.

Only 11 men in the history of the world had the opportunity to pray with the Son of God at this most crucial
time. Jesus was about to go to the cross to die for the sins
of the world, yet His disciples slept.

Jesus still has to do most things on earth without the
full participation of His Bride. She seems to lack "a wanting" of Him that would bring her to spiritual alertness.

Do not be too quick to criticize the disciples that failed
to come to the aid of their Savior. How many times have
we refused to respond to His call to prayer so we could get
a little more sleep?

When the groom in the "Song" comes into his garden, he calls for his bride. She was sleeping, but she does
hear his voice. She recognizes immediately that her groom
is wooing her. However, she hesitates and begins to give
excuses about why she will not respond instantly.

> "I have taken off my dress, How can I put it
> on {again?} I have washed my feet, How can I
> dirty them {again?}" (Song of Sol. 5:3).

Many of the following thoughts are taken from Dr.
Wade Taylor's book, *The Secret of the Stairs.*

In her day people went through quite a process of
cleaning themselves before going to bed. Most people wore
open sandals and the floors were primarily dirt. Therefore, washing their feet before they went to bed was quite

natural. Once she was clean and comfortable, the call came to her. It's not uncommon for us to be called out of our comfort zones as a test to see if our statements of love for the Lord are true.

When the bride hears the call, she hesitates and begins to give excuses about why she cannot respond to his call. Chapter five of the "Song" is a "looking back" at one of the lessons the bride had to learn in her process of abandonment. Ultimately she learns that when the groom calls, there can be no hesitation. As brides-to-be we have the same responsibility to respond to God when He calls us. Our hesitation comes from having lost a real sense of the holiness and majesty of our God. Who are we to factor in our own comfort in our response to God's call?

It seems today that the Church would like to become spiritual according to her own rules. We are in no position to decide the qualifications for spirituality. If we had our way, we would probably choose spirituality without inconvenience. It would be nice to be carnal one day and a spiritual giant the next, but it does not work that way. Spirituality comes through dying to your own plans, goals, and desires, so that you can take on His plans, goals, and desires.

"My beloved extended his hand through the opening, And my feelings were aroused for him" (Song of Sol. 5:4).

After some time of knocking and calling, the groom attempts to open the door to her chambers. In her day, doors did not have doorknobs or handles as we are accustomed to today. All they had were holes or openings that a person stuck their hand through from the outside so they could grab the latch that was on the inside.

When she saw him go to the trouble of attempting to open the door himself, she was aroused and decided to get out of bed to answer his call.

"I arose to open to my beloved; And my hands dripped with myrrh, And my fingers with liquid myrrh, On the handles of the bolt" (Song of Sol. 5:5).

In verse one, the groom talks about the myrrh and balsam that he had gathered. He was covered with an oil (anointing) from working in the vineyard. As she opened the door, her own hands were covered with the anointing that was on him. However, by the time she opened the door, he had given up trying to arouse her and had departed.

"I opened to my beloved, But my beloved had turned away {and} had gone! My heart went out {to him} as he spoke. I searched for him, but I did not find him; I called him but he did not answer me" (Song of Sol. 5:6).

Because the bride's carnal comforts were more important to her than His call, she loses a sense of his presence for some time. By the time she responds to him, he is gone. She then goes on a search for him and cannot find him for some time. She learns a great lesson here; there is to be no hesitation when the groom calls.

LOVING HIS PRESENCE

I once received a letter from a friend of mine who had just gotten married. As a single man, Jeff (not his real name) had a great heart for God. He had a wonderful prayer life. He fasted regularly. The presence of God was the most precious thing in his life. Eventually he met a Christian girl who caught his attention. After dating and praying together, they felt it was God's will for them to marry.

A few months after they married, I received a letter from him expressing some concern about his relationship with God.

He said, "Since I got married I really do not feel the presence of God in the same way I did while I was single. Why is this?"

I wrote back to him and explained a few things about the presence of God. I will summarize those thoughts here. The "Song" is about intimacy through separation. It describes the groom's attempt to get the bride to focus more on him than on her. The presence of God is best experienced through separation from the world. As a single man Jeff had separated himself in a unique way. He entered the garden often because his own comfort was not first on his list.

The reason Jeff felt as though he had lost some of the presence of God is best explained by looking at the subject of fasting. When we fast, we voluntarily separate ourselves from food. Because of that separation a person has the opportunity to experience the presence of God in wonderful ways while fasting. Once the fast is broken, a person goes back to eating. It is not uncommon, then, to feel that he has lost some of the closeness he had while fasting.

A single person is on a continual fast (or should be) regarding sex. Because of their separation from physical intimacy, spiritual intimacy becomes quite overwhelming and wonderful. When Jeff got married, he broke his sexual fast. Subsequently, he lost the sense of separation he had with the Lord as a single man. Therefore, he felt he had lost some of God's presence.

God does not expect any person to live on a continual fast of any type. He does instruct married couples in Corinth to fast from intimacy for a time. However, they are to eventually come back together so that temptation does not become too great (see I Cor. 7:5). He instructs them to fast for the sake of drawing close to him. Breaking a fast at its proper time is not really a problem with

God. In the same sense, it was not wrong for Jeff to get married. But, if we do not have a pattern of separation in our lives, we get to where the presence of God is no longer a major factor in our relationship with Him.

WHERE IS YOUR LOVE?

The bride was putting her own carnal comforts before her groom. Subsequently, when she finally did respond to him, and opened the door, he was gone. She then goes on a search for him throughout the land. She tries many different ways to enter back into his presence but without success.

Finally she is asked, "Where is your love?" (See Song of Sol. 6:1). Deep in her heart she knew all along where he was but was trying to find him other ways. She answers, "He's in the garden."

> "My beloved has gone down to his garden,
> To the beds of balsam, To pasture {his flock} in
> the gardens And gather lilies" (Song of Sol. 6:2).

Isn't it interesting how we will try to enter into a closeness with God without the separation that comes through prayer? We try to find God through church attendance, through tithing, through worship, and all the while we know that the presence of God is found in prayer. He's in the garden.

Hebrews 7:25 says, "He always lives to make intercession for them." Jesus is still in the garden of prayer. He ever lives to intercede. There is a presence of God in prayer that cannot be found in any other activity. When we pray, we enter into the garden with Him. We join Him in His work. If you feel you are away from the presence of God, it can be found again — in the garden of prayer.

It's interesting to compare the bride's experience to the disciples who were sleeping when Jesus called them to join Him in the Garden. Their own comfort was more important than His call. They failed to join Him during one of the most significant events in history. Subsequently, their spiritual insight was seriously affected. The disciples went into a time of spiritual blindness. They simply could not "see" what was going on during the crucifixion.

After the disciples lost the presence of God, they eventually were brought back into it through prayer. They found Him once again in the upper room on the Day of Pentecost. They were in prayer.

TWO HEARTS

It is easy to see the difference between the heart of the bride, and the heart of the daughters of Zion. The heart of the Bride lives for separation. It has a regular practice of prayer, fasting, and other spiritual disciplines. It is driven to the presence of her lover. The heart of the daughters of Zion (also known as the watchmen or the friends of the bride) is not drawn to the God of the work. It is drawn to the work of God.

The daughters measure their success by their skills and talents. Introspection is not a regular part of their lives. They are the type that is much more in love with their salvation rather than with their Savior. Is that not true of much of the Church today? We love our salvation. We love every aspect of it. We love eternal life. We love health and wealth. We love all of the benefits. Often our Savior must take a back seat to these things. We do not long for His presence. Subsequently, we lack spiritual disciplines.

If a church conducts a seminar on finances, big crowds will show up. If there is a seminar on healing, even bigger crowds show up. If there is a seminar on prayer, handfuls show up, if the weather permits.

When I talk to the Church about the inward life and

the need to seek God himself, the attitude of the daughters of Zion is, "Why are you making such a big deal out of nothing? I am not saved by how much I pray and fast." They lack a sense of wanting God. They only want their salvation.

This would be like a woman marrying a man because of the house and "goodies" he could provide her with. Men are presented with quite a dilemma. Most of them want, more than anything else, to be good providers, and yet once a wife becomes more taken up with his provisions than with him, he begins to withhold the very things he wants so desperately to provide.

TWO TYPES OF PRAY-ERS

There are two most common types of pray-ers. Philippians chapter four brings this out in a most interesting way.

SELF-SEEKING

Be anxious for nothing, but in everything by prayer and supplication with thanksgiving let your requests be made known to God. And the peace of God, which surpasses all comprehension, will guard your hearts and your minds in Christ Jesus (Phil. 4:6–7).

The self-seeking pray-er is the most common type. This kind of pray-er would fall into the category of the daughters of Zion. Their prayers are filled with concern over the cares of life. They make requests and supplications based on their personal comfort. They are seeking things from God rather than seeking God himself. Their life centers on the work of God.

Paul said it would be better to pray than to worry and that we should remember to thank God for all that He has done for us. Interestingly, even though their prayer life is based on what they can get from God, there is still a "peace of God" they experience (see Phil. 4:7). There is an anointing we can expect every time we pray. Even if all we do is pray for things, we are at least praying, which allows us to experience a certain presence of God or "peace of God."

GOD-SEEKING

The second type of pray-er is described in the next two verses.

> Finally, brethren, whatever is true, whatever is honorable, whatever is right, whatever is pure, whatever is lovely, whatever is of good repute, if there is any excellence and if anything worthy of praise, let your mind dwell on these things. The things you have learned and received and heard and seen in me, practice these things; and the God of peace will be with you (Phil. 4:8–9).

Paul first talks about the pray-er who seeks things from God. Then he concludes his thoughts by saying in essence, "Do what I do." What does Paul do? He seeks God himself. He gives himself to whatever is true, honorable, right, pure, etc. These things describe qualities of the Lord himself. He says, "Let your mind dwell on these things." In other words, be consumed with the Lord himself, and the "God of peace" will be with you. This describes the heart of the Bride. Her heart is taken up with Him. She is more in love with her Savior than with her salvation.

The bride experiences the "God of peace" (see Phil. 4:9), while the daughters experience the "peace of God." There is a world of difference between these two things. However, this also presents a problem. We never hunger for anything we have never tasted.

I have had many opportunities to teach pastors'

schools in many different countries. In some of those countries I have been offered some "interesting" foods to eat. In Africa they eat fried grasshoppers. It's quite common to find little boys walking around with plastic bags full of live grasshoppers for sale. My host bought a bag of them once and prepared them for us. All you do is pull the legs and wings off and throw them into the frying pan. They make their own oil. It's really quite "fascinating." They are served in large bowls much the same way we serve popcorn.

I can honestly say that before I ever ate a fried grasshopper, I never did crave one. There was never a time that I can remember saying to my wife, "Honey, I feel like grasshoppers tonight." You never hunger for something you have never tasted.

It seems most of the Church today is content with the peace of God having never tasted of the God of peace. We are to taste and see that the Lord is good.

The bride in the "Song" reveals this dilemma. Though she is called the "bride," she is still in a rather carnal state. That should give all of us hope. God is not requiring perfection from any of us before we can be classified as part of the bride. He is simply looking for hearts that want Him.

When the knock first came on her door the bride hesitated because her prayer life at that point was still based on her need. From her perspective, she did not really need to respond because it appeared that all of her needs were currently met. She was still very much in that mode of seeking things from God rather than seeking God. Subsequently, when she did respond, the anointing that was on him gets on her hands. This is like the peace of God. It's like getting God himself on you.

If she had pursued the Lord himself, things would have been different. Then when the knock came to her door, she would have cast off all of her carnal comforts and responded immediately. Then when she opened the door, the "God of Peace" would have been there. The "peace of God" is like getting God on some of you while the "God of peace" is like getting God himself all over you.

SEEK MY FACE

"You have made my heart beat faster, my sister, {my} bride; You have made my heart beat faster with a single {glance} of your eyes, With a single strand of your necklace" (Song of Sol. 4:9).

In this setting Solomon is expressing the infatuation he has over his love. They have just come from his secret place and are now descending back down the mountain. The secret place is the place of prayer. It is the place where we hear His voice and He hears our voice. It is the place where we behold each other. Solomon's bride must have been gazing into his eyes, which prompted his statement, "You have made my heart beat faster with a single (glance) of your eyes."

Isn't it interesting to think that we, the bride of Christ, could make the heart of Jesus flutter by simply turning our eyes to His? A single glance did it for Solomon. There is something special about looking someone in the eyes. There is also something intimate about looking someone in the eyes. What would happen if you were to turn to the person closest to you and simply gaze into their eyes for several moments? It would be very difficult unless you had a proper relationship with them. It's much easier to look someone in the nose. It's not nearly as pleasant but it is easier.

When two people's eyes meet something happens. They have made a type of contact. When someone looks us in the eye, it shows that we have his or her attention. That is what this is all about. When you are pursuing someone, you want their attention. Shortly after I met Lou Ann, the woman who eventually became my wife, we departed for the summer. We met in Bible college and had dated only a couple of times when the summer break came, and Lou was leaving to counsel in a kid's camp while I was staying behind to work a job.

I was not quite sure how she felt about me yet. I was very sure of how I felt about her. I had already flipped over her. You must understand, this was many years ago when I could flip. Today I would have to flop over somebody, and that would not be a good way to start a relationship. You can imagine my joy when I got a letter from her and in it she said, "I have thought about you a lot." That was great! I had her attention. I wanted her thinking about me. I did not want her to think about others.

TWO TYPES OF SEEKERS

In my first book, *Prayer Can Change Your Marriage*, I talked about a favorite illustration of mine that I call "two types of seekers." I am going to reiterate it here because it is so fitting.

The Bible shows that there are two types of seekers. There are those who look to the hands and those who look to the eyes. Beggars look to the hands. If a beggar has ever approached you, you probably found that he was most interested in your hand. He wanted to see what you could pull out of your pocket to give to him. They seek things much like the first type of pray-er mentioned in Philippians 4:6.

The second type of seeker is a lover. Lovers look to the eyes. The person in love needs only one thing: to know the one he loves, loves him in return so he looks to the eyes because the eyes tell the story. Seekers who are lovers are more interested in the other person than they are themselves. They are not just interested in what they can get from the other person. They reflect the second type of pray-er found in Philippians 4:8.

Throughout the Old Testament especially, we find the Lord admonishing us to seek His face. He says in essence, "If you love me, seek my face." Seeking the face of God indicates a pursuit of Him rather than just seeking things from him.

> Behold, the LORD'S hand is not so short
> That it cannot save; Neither is His ear so dull
> That it cannot hear (Isa. 59:1).

Often the Lord refers to the fact that His hand is not short. In other words, God can reach us with all of our needs. Do not worry about His hands. Do not worry about your needs. Never let the bulk of your prayer life center around the cares of this life. The Lord's hand is not shortened. He can reach you with your needs no matter where you are. Seek His face.

The bride was being taken through the process of giving up more and more of her life. She was being taught that seeking the face of her love would ultimately meet all the needs of her life. I sought my wife's face. I wanted her. I ended up with her hand in marriage. In other words, I sought her and gained not only her, but everything she possessed, also. Seek the face of God. If you do, you will end up with His hand in marriage.

CHAPTER SIX

THE BRIDE VS. THE DAUGHTERS

As we go through the "Song," we begin to see a distinct difference between the bride and the daughters of Zion. As we stated in the previous chapter, the daughters just do not see what the bride sees. How is it that the bride can see more clearly than the daughters? It is not because of some kind of elitism. Everyone has an opportunity to develop in the same characteristics as the bride. However, some Christians simply choose not to pursue spiritual things.

In chapter 3 of the "Song," we have a great example of this. The bride is expressing her heart by describing how she longs for Him. When she encounters the watchmen (daughters), they are busy about the work of God and cannot appreciate her desire.

"On my bed night after night I sought him Whom my soul loves; I sought him but did not find him. 'I must arise now and go about the city; In the streets and in the squares I must seek him whom my soul loves.' I sought him but did not find him. The watchmen who make the rounds in the city found me, {And I said,} 'Have you seen him whom my soul loves?' Scarcely had I left them When I found him whom my soul loves; I held on to him and would not let him go" (Song of Sol. 3:1–4).

Though the bride was going through a spiritually dry time (she sought Him but did not find Him), she never gave up in her pursuit of Him. Those who hunger and thirst shall be filled. Because of her undying drive and desire for Him, she eventually finds him.

It seems that the bride has a revelation that the daughters lack. She appears to "see" what the others do not see. Her revelation has caused her to develop a pursuit of Him, understanding that the work of God will ultimately be accomplished through her pursuit of Him.

WHEN HE APPEARS

Dear friends, now we are children of God, and what we will be has not yet been made known. But we know that *when he appears,* we shall be like him, for we shall see him as he is (1 John 3:2;NIV, emphasis added).

This verse has traditionally been viewed from the context of the Lord's return to earth. Though that is probably the most accurate application of this verse, we need to consider another aspect of it, also. It's true that one day Jesus is going to appear on earth in His second coming. However, Jesus is already appearing on earth every day in other ways. Our Lord's appearances today are what we call revelations. These revelations (appearances) come in many different forms.

In the Old Testament we see His appearances through many different theophanies. A theophany is a visible appearance of God, generally in human form, though some accounts record the appearance as an angel. One such event is found in Genesis 32. In this account Jacob was by himself in the wilderness when a "man" appeared and they began to wrestle.

"Then Jacob was left alone, and a man wrestled with him until daybreak" (Gen. 32:24). Four verses later the "man" identifies himself as God: "Then the man said, 'Your name will no longer be Jacob, but Israel, because you have struggled with God and with men and have overcome' " (Gen. 32:28).

Genesis 22 records another theophany when Abraham was about to sacrifice his own son. "But the angel of the LORD called to him from heaven and said, 'Abraham! Abraham!' 'Here I am,' he replied," (Gen. 22:11). Here the appearing was as "the angel of the Lord." Though this event records that it was an angel, the next verse reveals to us that it was the Lord himself:

> "Do not lay a hand on the boy," he said. "Do not do anything to him. Now I know that you fear God, because you have not withheld from me your son, your only son" (Gen. 22:12;NIV).

God had asked Abraham to sacrifice his son. When He saw that Abraham was going to do it, He appeared to him. Though He appeared as an angel he said, "You have not withheld from *me* your son."

In the early days of humanity God often appeared to men and even talked with them (see Gen. 18). However, this was all before man had the written Word. This was also before the incarnation and the giving of the Holy Spirit. The Old Testament was very physical, whereas the New Testament is much more spiritual. In the Old Testament men had to see God because they did not yet have the indwelling Holy Spirit. That is a part of the reason the miracles in the Old Testament were on such a grand scale.

Now that the Holy Spirit has made His abode in the hearts of man, it seems that the "appearing" requires a new set of prerequisites. A revelation of Christ requires Christ-like qualities to gain it. In other words, we must first develop in the character of Christ before we can see Christ today. Obedience to the commands of God is the first prerequisite. As we follow the Lord in obedience, we develop in His character. Character gives us the ability to "see" what the Lord is truly like.

> Whoever has my commands and obeys them, he is the one who loves me. He who loves me will be loved by my Father, and I too will love him and show myself to him (John 14:21;NIV).

The Son of God still appears regularly to men. However, the depth of the "appearing" is based on the spiritual condition of a man's heart before the revelation takes place. The depth of a man's obedience is the barometer of his spiritual condition.

> With the kind Thou dost show Thyself kind; With the blameless Thou dost show Thyself blameless; With the pure Thou dost show Thyself pure (Ps. 18:25–26).

REVELATION OF CHARACTER

Many times God appears in some form of His character. I remember watching a TV news program that was recording the events surrounding our military men coming back from the Persian Gulf conflict in the early 1990s. One of our aircraft carriers had just ported in Florida and the soldiers were walking down the plank onto American soil for the first time in months. As their feet touched the ground each man's family would break through the barriers which kept the crowd back and run. With outstretched arms and tear-filled eyes, they would hug each other's neck and weep for joy.

My own eyes were welling up with tears as I was watching these men. They would hold wives with one arm and take their children in their other arm. It seems all they could do was kiss their cheeks and look at them. Apparently they could not get enough of each other. It was a wonderful display of love and emotion. Suddenly the Lord spoke to me and said, "This is a revelation of Me." Immediately I realized what God was saying to me. Outward displays of true love are disclosures of who God is. God is simply trying to get across to His people what He is like. All kindnesses, all mercies, all longsufferings, are manifestations of God himself. Emotional experiences come from being in the presence of God. We think they come from our love for others when in reality our love for others is simply a manifestation of God himself.

Unless we have developed the same quality in which He appears, we simply cannot "see" Him. We see Him when we are like Him. In other words, we know that when He appears we shall be like Him, for we shall see Him as He is, when *we are* as He is.

Those who do not know Him, also see Him as He is, when we are as He is. God reveals himself to us through our own character development. Then He reveals himself to those who do not yet house His Spirit, through our outward display of His character. Jesus came to earth to reveal His Father to a people who did not know Him. He revealed the Father through His great acts of mercy and love, culminating in His own death. Until we develop in His character, we fail in our own "revelation" of who He is and what He wants to do for others.

The Bride is the Bride because of what she "sees," not because God has chosen her over others. The daughters simply do not see because they have not developed in character. The Bride "sees" according to the character of Christ she has developed in.

What we are dealing with is something much more important and of much more value than just gaining more revelation-knowledge. What we need to be seeking is more of God himself, not just more knowledge about Him. God is love, and without us operating in that Spirit (love), there is no means to grasp what God's Spirit reveals to us.

Consider the following verses in light of this:

> But when he, the Spirit of truth, comes, he will guide you into all truth. He will not speak on his own; he will speak only what he hears, and he will tell you what is yet to come. He will bring glory to me by taking from what is mine and making it known to you. All that belongs to the Father is mine. That is why I said the Spirit will take from what is mine and make it known to you (John 16:13–15;NIV).

The Spirit of God is the revelator. The Spirit must make things known to us. If a man is not operating according to the true nature of God's spirit, he cannot gain any true revelation of the nature of Christ. This is the basic problem with the daughters. They operate out of a religious spirit rather than from a heart of desire.

THE PURE HEART

Consider the following verse:

> And now, dear children, continue in him, so that when he appears we may be confident and unashamed before him at his coming (1 John 2:28;NIV).

One day we are going to stand before Him. If a person were given the option of either standing before the Lord this very minute, or an hour from now, what do you suppose he would choose? If it were me, I would take the hour. I would not need it to secure my salvation, I'm a Christian, but I would like to pray about a few things before standing before Him. I would like to pray about all the things that I did not do for Him. I would like to repent over the areas of my life that I really did not allow Him to conform. I would like to get in "one last prayer" for my lost loved ones. In essence, I would ask God to forgive me for not fully obeying Him. However, this verse gives us great hope when it says, "If we continue in Him we will not be ashamed at His coming."

What does it mean to continue (live) in Him? The answer can be found in the same chapter of I John.

Whoever claims to live in him must walk as Jesus did (1 John 2:6;NIV).

Walking as Jesus walked has a purifying effect of us. There would be no shame at His second coming if a person walked as Jesus walked. Do you see the connection between His second coming (appearing) and the way He appears today? Our obedience, before His appearing, plays a significant part.

Now we must reconsider our opening verse:

Dear friends, now we are children of God, and what we will be has not yet been made known. But we know that when he appears, we shall be like him, for we shall see him as he is (1 John 3:2;NIV).

We must live with the hope that when He appears we shall be like Him. This means more than us instantly conforming to His character at the time of His coming. This verse is telling us that the "depth" or "impact" of

His appearing is decided by our Christ-likeness before His appearing. The next verse brings this out:

> Everyone who has this hope in him purifies himself, just as he is pure (1 John 3:3;NIV).

Everyone who has the hope of being like Him when He appears, has that hope, because of his or her pure heart. When you live with the hope of being like Him, you purify your own heart in the process because you walk as He walked. Subsequently, you purify yourself just as *He* is pure. It takes purity of heart to be able to "see." Revelation comes through *doing* (obedience), which results in *being* (Christ-likeness). Everyone who has the hope of seeing Him when He appears, becomes as pure as He is. The reason they have that hope is because of their obedience to Him.

Jesus appears through His Word. Jesus appears through our worship of Him, and He appears in our prayers to Him. However, Jesus does not just appear because we do these things. He appears when we do these things with a right spirit. David prayed in Psalm 51:10:

> Create in me a clean heart, O God, And renew a steadfast spirit within me.

When our heart is pure, our spirit is "right." Without a "right spirit," Jesus cannot appear in His truest form, though we spend hours in prayer, the word, and worship. When He appears it's because we pray, read, and worship in a right spirit. A right spirit is developed through submitting to His will and Word. If we are submitted to His Word, then we must conform to its guidelines.

As we obey God, we purify our hearts. To the purified heart, He appears. The depth of His appearing is according to the depth of our obedience. Not until a person gives himself to prayer does he "see." Time in the presence of God is the primary method of developing in His character.

JUST DON'T GET IT!

This is all about developing in the character of Christ. Charles Finney used to say, "Benevolent thoughts do not constitute prayer." There is nothing passive about true prayer. It is purposeful and deliberate.

Smith Wigglesworth, a great evangelist from the past, was famous for saying, "I cannot remember ever setting aside 30 minutes for a prayer time. However, I also cannot remember ever going 30 minutes without praying." People are always quoting that to me because I have a strong emphasis on people setting aside time daily to spend in prayer. However, I have a personal struggle with that particular approach to prayer.

A minister acquaintance of mine wrote some memoirs before his death concerning his relationship with God. He died of cancer and had time to write down some final thoughts that he felt summed up his life and service to God. He made an interesting comment about his prayer life. He said in essence, "I was not the type of person that spent large amounts of time in prayer. I cannot say that I rose early each day and had a consecrated prayer time. However, I was in constant communion with the Lord throughout each day." That is not an exact quotation but it captures the essence of his remarks.

First of all, I find it quite interesting that he felt the need to justify his lack of specific prayer times. Have you ever noticed that no one feels compelled to justify too much prayer? Secondly, it typifies a "daughter of Zion" lifestyle. The memoirs of a bride would talk about great times of communion, in the secret place, with her Lord. My friend was one taken up with the work of the Lord rather than the Lord of the work.

How would similar words sound to your spouse? Suppose you were dying and you had time to assess your relationship with your spouse. If you said something similar to what my friend said about his relationship with Jesus it would sound somewhat like this: *Honey, I was not the type of person to spend much time with you. I can however, honestly say that rarely did a moment go by that I was not thinking of you.* How would that make your mate feel? Something would be missing in that relationship. They just don't seem to get it.

When we think back to the garden scene, Jesus is praying. The weight of the world is upon Him. He is sweating drops of blood. He struggles to his feet and pulls himself to where His disciples are sleeping. He says to them, "Could you join me for just one hour?" His disciples squint through their sleepy eyes and watch Him walk back to the place of prayer, alone. This does not happen just once. This happens three times.

Not much has changed today, has it? Jesus is still in the place of prayer while most of His disciples sleep. Our thoughts are with Him. Why, we would never think of going through a day without giving much thought to Him, but don't ask us to actually join Him in the garden. We are much too tired for that.

The message of the "Song" is quite simple. Jesus wants us to join Him in the secret place. He has come into His garden, and He says, "Could you not tarry with me one hour?" The bride will do so. The daughters will continue to justify their lack of desire. They just don't get it!

CHAPTER SEVEN

THE PEARLS
OF INTIMACY

"Oh that you were like a brother to me Who nursed at my mother's breasts. {If} I found you outdoors, I would kiss you; No one would despise me, either" (Song of Sol. 8:1).

The bride wishes for a constant intimacy and freedom with her intended. She was already betrothed to him, but the nuptials had not been solemnized or published. Therefore, she was obliged to be shy and show very little public affection.

Every relationship has hidden aspects to it that are to remain hidden. Yet within the heart of lovers is a desire to let the world know of the beauty of the one their heart has gone out to. In our opening verse the bride is simply echoing the sentiments of the king when he revealed who he was to her on Mount Hermon.

He said in Song of Solomon 4:12, "You are a garden locked up, my sister, my bride; you are a spring enclosed, a sealed fountain" (NIV).

Once she agrees to be his wife, he wants the whole

world to know of her beauty, but currently she was a garden locked up. They both long for a freedom to express their love openly. However, the bride was being observed by the daughters of Zion and others who did not understand intimacy. Proper protocol demanded that they not have any public displays of affection. Therefore, she expresses that it would be much better if he were like a brother to her. If he were her brother, she could openly express her love and no one would think anything of it.

THE PEARL OF GREAT PRICE

And upon finding one pearl of great value, he went and sold all that he had, and bought it (Matt. 13:46).

After the Mount Hermon experience and discovering who her mystery lover was, the bride becomes quite taken up with His affections. She now realizes that she has discovered her King, her Savior, her salvation, her pearl of great price! However, she has also learned the hard way that those around her do not fully understand her relationship with Him.

In Matthew 7:6 we learn another lesson about pearls:

Do not give what is holy to dogs, and do not throw your pearls before swine, lest they trample them under their feet, and turn and tear you to pieces.

Do not throw your pearls before swine. If you throw a handful of pearls into a pigsty, they will simply stare at them and eventually trample them into the mud. It is impossible for the pigs to give an appropriate response because they cannot understand the value of pearls. The value of pearls is not within their realm of reasoning.

The bride had thrown out many pearls to the watchmen in chapter 5 of the "Song," and they trampled her statements to the ground. She was on a search for him and was asking for their help when she began to express his beauty:

> "My beloved is dazzling and ruddy, Outstanding among ten thousand. His head is {like} gold, pure gold; His locks are {like} clusters of dates, {And} black as a raven. His eyes are like doves, Beside streams of water, Bathed in milk, {And} reposed in {their} setting" (Song of Sol. 5:10–12).

The watchmen were far more interested in the work of God than they were in the God of the work. Subsequently, when she describes His beauty, they cannot relate. It makes no sense to them. They even ask her why she thinks her lover is better than theirs (see details of this in chapter 8).

The bride knows she cannot cast her pearls again so she fantasizes of what she could do publicly if he were her brother. Is that not true of us today? Would it not be wonderful to be able to fully express to an unenlightened world and Church what intimacy with Christ means to you? But how could such a thing be put into words? It cannot be. At least not now. Maybe we will be able to express this when the marriage of the King of kings to the bride of Christ is complete. Maybe then we will be able to express openly and fully the intimacies of our relationship with Him. Maybe.

I find it quite interesting that Matthew 7:6 associates holiness with pearls:

> Do not give what is holy to dogs, and do not throw your pearls before swine.

Holiness is a separation. To live a holy life, you must live separate from the world. Separation denotes privacy. Therefore, the admonition to us is this: Do not share with others the private aspects of your relationship with Christ for those things are holy.

THE EMBRACE OF THE SPIRIT

"Let his left hand be under my head, And
his right hand embrace me" (Song of Sol. 8:3).

The bride gives us a glimpse of what took place in
the garden, the secret place or the place of prayer. She
talks of him holding her and embracing her. Solomon must
have learned many things from the psalms his father wrote.
Solomon was a man of great wisdom. Surely a part of his
wisdom must have come through the study of the God-
inspired words of his shepherd father.

King David had an intimacy with the Father that
we all should seek. In one of his psalms he wrote that
when God held him (David) with His right hand, it
caused his soul to follow hard after God (see Ps. 63:8). It
seems that Solomon used this technique on Abishag. Two
different times the bride talks of Solomon's left hand
holding her head and his right hand embracing her. She
is therefore empowered by his spirit (see Song of Sol.
2:6, 8:3).

The embrace of the spirit gives us the ability to overcome the world. What the bride is expressing is the empowering that comes through intimacy. Does anything give
a marriage more drive and desire than intimacy? Intimacy
becomes the empowering of the spirit. It is the glue of the
relationship. It is the drawing. Intimacy causes one's mind
to be fully occupied with the one you love.

DO NOT AWAKEN!

"I charge you, O daughters of Jerusalem,
that ye stir not up, nor awake {my} love, until he
please" (Song of Sol. 8:4;KJV).

The bride charged those about her to take heed of
doing anything to interrupt the pleasing communion she
now had with her beloved. She had done this once before,

THE PEARLS OF INTIMACY

when he strengthened and comforted her with his presence (see Song of Sol. 2:7).

The Church charges all her children to never do anything to provoke Christ to withdraw, which we are very prone to do. Why would we ever want to affront Him? Why would we want to be such enemies to ourselves?

I have had times in prayer when the presence of God was so strong, so real, and so soothing, that the last thing I would have ever considered would be to stop praying. When we arouse Him before His time by cutting our prayer time short, we are saying, "I am weary of Christ's presence."

> He couches, he lies down as a lion, And as a
> lion, who dares rouse him? (Num. 24:9).

Who dares rouse the Lion of Judah? There is an old saying that goes like this: "It's not nice to mess with Mother Nature." The idea behind the saying is that Mother Nature has great power, and you don't want to do anything to disturb her or you may pay a price for it. Jesus is the Lion of Judah. Who dares rouse a sleeping lion? If you are in the embrace of Christ, the Lion of Judah, why would you want to rouse Him?

Have you ever fallen asleep in the arms of your spouse? There is something very tender about sleeping in the embrace of your mate. Just about the time my wife is about to fall asleep in my embrace, my arm that is under her falls asleep and I must move it. Moving my arm out from under her awakens her and ruins the moment.

The bride is in the embrace of her love and she says to the daughters around her, "Do not awaken my love until he pleases." She says in essence, "I am completely content in His embrace. I do not want this time to be cut short by one moment."

If only we could grasp the tenderness of prayer. Prayer is a giving of ourselves to our love. It is a time He is to be in complete control of. We are to be in a position of surrender. We hear His voice and He hears our voice. We behold Him and He beholds us. It's a very delicate time. I personally struggle with the militant spirit that is coming out of the spiritual warfare camp that espouses a demanding type of praying. The battle is the Lord's. I do not even need to address the enemy while I am in the garden of prayer. When we are in His embrace, we are free of satanic attack.

A YOUNG STAG

Periodically, Solomon had to go back to his palace to take care of business — after all he is still the king. There are several times when we see the bride looking for her "shepherd," but she cannot seem to find him. These "searchings" all took place before he revealed who he really was.

> "Listen! My beloved! Behold, he is coming, Climbing on the mountains, Leaping on the hills! My beloved is like a gazelle or a young stag. Behold, he is standing behind our wall, He is looking through the windows, He is peering through the lattice" (Song of Sol. 2:8–9).

In these verses we read of an account where Solomon is returning after having been gone for some time. She sees him climbing and leaping and looking through the windows, seeking her out. What she is seeing is a young man in love. He is like a gazelle or young stag (deer). When young men are in love, they have much energy. They can run through a troop and leap over a wall. They can climb mountains and leap on the hills. Unfortunately for women, men who are over 40 seem to only have enough energy to stand and look at mountains. They ride on air-conditioned buses and gaze out the window at them.

The important thing to grasp here is that the energy a man in love has comes through anticipating being with the one he loves. This is what attracts the bride. She knows that his energy, his life, is coming from his love for her.

Two different times in the "Song" the bride encourages her lover to be a "young stag" (see Song of Sol. 2:17, 8:14). This could be a great lesson for all husbands. Our wives want us to be exhilarated with their love. Solomon must have learned this lesson from Abishag at one point because he gives some advice on this subject:

> {As} a loving hind and a graceful doe, Let her breasts satisfy you at all times; Be exhilarated always with her love. For why should you, my son, be exhilarated with an adulteress, And embrace the bosom of a foreigner? (Prov. 5:19–20).

Take some advice from Solomon, the wisest man who ever lived. In these verses he tells husbands that each of us has, in our own wives, everything we will ever need. Embrace your wife. Do not be taken up with an adulteress. If a man's wife is not responding to him, it's because we have ceased to be that "young stag." A woman knows when her husband is taken up with her or when he is taken up with looking at other women.

LEANING ON HER BELOVED

In chapter 3 of the "Song" we get a glimpse of the wedding ceremony.

> Behold, it is the {traveling} couch of Solomon; Sixty mighty men around it, Of the mighty men of Israel. All of them are wielders of the sword, Expert in war; Each man has his sword at his side, {Guarding} against the terrors of the night. King Solomon has made for himself a sedan chair from the timber of Lebanon. He made its posts of silver, Its back of gold {And} its seat of purple fabric, {With} its interior

lovingly fitted out By the daughters of Jerusalem. Go forth, O daughters of Zion, And gaze on King Solomon with the crown With which his mother has crowned him On the day of his wedding, And on the day of his gladness of heart (Song of Sol. 3:7–11).

Delmer Guynes says, "The royal carriage and the elite bodyguard are in evidence, but the pomp and ceremony are displaced by a tender display of love between the king and the Shunammite queen. She is seen in a moment of loving dependence upon the one who has transformed her life."[1] The daughters of Zion were watching both the king and the bride. They had been carefully assessing her relationship with the shepherd from a distance. They knew her to be a mere caretaker of the vineyard, and yet there was something different about her since she met him. Now they see her walking out of the wilderness coming into their own village leaning on him: "Who is this coming up from the wilderness, leaning on her beloved?" (Song of Sol. 8:5). Guynes continues, "The image of Abishag leaning lovingly on the King of the Realm must have awed her homefolk at Shunem. How could this have happened to the little shepherdess who was so often the object of ridicule and mistreatment by her family and friends?"[2]

THE APOSTLE JOHN

There was reclining on Jesus' breast one of
His disciples, whom Jesus loved (John 13:23).

John, like the bride, also leaned upon the King. John was one of three that shared in another Mount Hermon experience called the Transfiguration of Christ. John saw Jesus in His royal robes of pure white. It's possible that John then began to understand who this simple carpenter really was. His carpenter garb was simply a disguise. This one who simply showed up out of nowhere and began to show interest in him was really the King of kings!

When we read the phrase, "His disciple, whom Jesus loved," it is possible to think that Jesus loved John and not the others. It would be equally easy to think that Jesus loves the Bride and not the daughters of Zion. However, that would be contrary to the verse that says, "God is love." God loves all people equally. God loves the daughters as much as He does the Bride. Those who make up the Bride are those who have a heart that wants God. They understand intimacy. It seems that the call to intimacy goes out to all believers. However, not all believers feel the need to respond to it. They fail to understand the importance of intimacy with Him.

This phrase is speaking about John's intimacy with Christ. John cultivated an intimacy with his Lord that the other disciples had not yet come into. He developed the characteristics of the Bride before the other disciples.

Because of putting Jesus first, John experienced many significant "firsts" in his life. He was the first one to the empty tomb (see John 20:4). He was the first one to recognize Jesus after the resurrection (see John 21:7). John was taken up with his Lord.

Of the 12 original apostles, one of them was interested in the kingdom of the world — Judas. Ten of them were interested in the kingdom of God. John, however, was interested in the King himself. In that, he differed from the others similarly to how the Bride differs from the daughters of Zion.

LAY YOUR HEAD ON MY CHEST

John leaned on his beloved in the same way the bride in the Song leaned on her beloved. I have a friend who once went on a personal retreat to seek the Lord. He spent three days praying and fasting in a cabin in northern Wisconsin.

He told me that on the third day he experienced something that had never happened to him before or since.

As he was in prayer the Lord spoke to him and said, "Lay your head on my chest. I want you to hear my heart beat. I want you to hear me breathe. I want you to understand that every beat of my heart beats just for you. Every breath I breathe, I breathe just for you." He went on to say that it was a most humbling experience that had a deep impact on his life.

MY SHEEP KNOW MY VOICE

When he puts forth all his own, he goes before them, and the sheep follow him because they know his voice (John 10:4).

Those who know His voice are those who can hear His heartbeat. Those who hear His heartbeat are those who have an intimacy with Him. Do you hear the heartbeat of God? Many pastors are so obsessed with how to grow their churches that the obvious passes them by. What is the heartbeat of God concerning His church? Is it numbers or is it intimacy? If it were simply numbers, then the "Song" would be about the daughters of Zion instead of the Bride. It would be about His pleasure with those who do not seek Him, rather than the Bride. To understand the voice of God, one must hear His heartbeat. The one whom Jesus loved leaned upon the bosom of Christ.

When my son was very young, one of my favorite things to do was to lie on the couch with him. I would have him lay on me with his head on my chest. There is something very special about having your child lay their head on you. As I would hold his head close to my heart, it was almost as if I were transferring my life into him. I believe Jesus would have each of us develop that type of intimacy with Him. He longs to transfer His life into us. He longs to have us hear his heartbeat.

CHAPTER EIGHT

DOES HE HAVE
THE BRIDE?

"I am my beloved's" (Song of Sol. 7:10).

When the bride said, "I am my beloved's," she was expressing her complete surrender to the groom. She said in essence, "He has me. He has complete rule in my life." It had taken the groom a considerable amount of time to bring his bride to this place of surrender.

If we compare this event to a New Testament event we can gain some interesting insight. John the Baptist and his disciples had been preaching repentance for some time trying to prepare his followers for the coming Messiah. When Jesus did come on the scene John's disciples were not quite sure if He truly was the Son of God. At one point they came to John and asked if Jesus was truly the Messiah. John's answer to their query is quite interesting. In John 3:29 we read of his response to them: He who has the bride is the bridegroom. John could also have answered their question by asking some questions himself, "Does He have the Bride? Do the multitudes follow Him? If He has the Bride He is the Bridegroom."

John was most likely thrilled with the fact that the Messiah had finally come. He had been preparing the way for Him for years. He lived a separated life in the desert. He prayed, he fasted, he preached, he baptized — and now the Son of God had actually come. John was preparing to decrease so that the Son of God could increase.

Did He have the Bride? There would be no contest at all if Satan was as truthful with us as God is. If Jesus and Satan stood side by side and told us exactly what they had planned for our future, which one would end up with the Bride?

Consider this scenario:

Jesus and Satan stand before all the world and tell of their individual plans for mankind. First, Jesus says, "My plan is to prosper you. It is to give you eternal peace, love, joy, and happiness. If you surrender your heart to me, I will possess you and be with you forever."

Then Satan stands up and speaks to the same crowd and says, "My plan for you is torment. There will be loneliness, bitterness, unforgiveness, and hatred. If you surrender your heart to me, I will possess you and give you much grief. By the way, it will never end."

Which one would gain the bride? It would seem that every man alive would choose Jesus once he fully understood the plan of both Jesus and Satan.

KINGSHIP IS A MATTER OF POSSESSION

He who has the Bride is the Bridegroom. You could also say, he who has the queen is the king. This is a matter of possession. God wants to possess us, so does Satan. Kingship is decided by the one who wins the heart of the Bride.

When Adonijah, Solomon's older brother, came to Bathsheba to see if he could gain the hand of Abishag in marriage, he knew exactly what he was doing. In the normal tradition, the kingdom was handed to the oldest son of the king. If Abishag, Solomon's queen, would have become the wife of Adonijah, he could have won the respect of the people of the land and subsequently the kingship. When Bathsheba asked Solomon to allow Abishag to become his brother's wife, he erupted into a rage that cost Adonijah his life. Solomon knew it was not just a matter of losing his wife. It also meant losing his position as king. To lose the heart of the queen is to lose one's ability to reign.

The bride represents the people. The one the bride runs to is king. This is why the bride's prayer in the first chapter of the Song of Songs is so significant:

> "Draw me after you {and} let us run {together!} The king has brought me into his chambers. We will rejoice in you and be glad; We will extol your love more than wine. Rightly do they love you" (Song of Sol. 1:4).

When she expressed her desire to run with the King and to be brought into his chambers she was proclaiming Him Lord over her life. There is no lordship without possession. The King of kings reigns only in the heart of the man who has surrendered to Him. Though He is the King of kings, without the surrender of the heart there is no rulership, no lordship. This puts an incredible amount of responsibility on the bride. In a certain sense, the bride determines who the ruler of the land is.

If all men would surrender their hearts to Christ, this would be the kingdom of God on earth because Jesus would occupy each heart. Subsequently, Satan would have no place to rule. Proverbs 14:28 brings this out:

> In a multitude of people is a king's glory,
> but in the dearth of people is a prince's ruin.

Who wants to be the king of the dirt? Suppose you were crowned king of a particular country that had no people. Everyday you would rise and look out over your land and state to yourself that you are the king of everything you see. Without subjects, your kingship would mean nothing. Jesus does not want to be King over the mountains. He wants to be King of our hearts. When the King has the multitudes He is glorified but a prince is ruined in the dearth of people. The word "dearth" can simply be translated "cessation" or "end." The cessation of the prince's rule in the hearts of his subjects ruins him. This is most appropriate when we compare Jesus, the King of kings, to Satan, the prince of the power of the air (see Eph. 2:2).

A large population that reveres the King of kings brings much glory to Him. Simply by honoring the King of kings we ruin the prince of the power of the air. This would simplify the complicated mess we have made out of spiritual warfare. Spiritual warfare tactics could be simplified by one simple truth. If you want to ruin the enemy, bring all men to Jesus.

HIGH PRIEST OF THE HOME?

How does a man reign in his family as the high priest? He reigns by possession. Many men live their lives without ever possessing the heart of their wives. They have the position as the head of the house by virtue of a God-given right. However, if they do not possess the heart of their wives, they have position without possession. Jesus has been appointed the head of the Church. Therefore, He has the position. But, if He does not possess His bride, through her surrender to Him, He has very little influence though He is the King of kings.

If Satan possessed the heart of every man on earth this would be his kingdom even though Jesus is the one true King over everything. That is exactly what Adonijah was up to. He knew that Solomon was the appointed king, but if he gained the heart of the bride he could overrule the designated king.

LOWLINESS

Solomon's approach to winning the heart of Abishag reveals the lowliness of Christ. Solomon was king of the realm. He could have anything his heart desired. He could have made any request of anybody, and it would have been granted. However, he chose to humble himself and win her heart instead.

Christ is King of all creation! He is the one and only King, yet He does not demand the love of His bride. He gently woos her. He came to her dressed as an equal to give her an option. If she chooses to submit her heart, He gains rulership. If she chooses not to submit, Jesus does not react out of anger, He simply continues to pray.

THREE POSITIONS

As the bride was taken through the process of abandonment or complete possession, she proclaimed where she was at in the process three different times. Wade Taylor calls this her "three statements of position."

POSITION ONE

Her first position is stated in Song of Solomon 2:16:

"My beloved is mine, and I am his; He pastures {his flock} among the lilies."

This really is an expression of immaturity. She had herself before Him. She said, "He is mine!" It is not atypical for a person to begin their relationship with Christ from this position. When people first meet Christ, they are called "babes" — babes in Christ.

First Corinthians 3:1 says, "And I, brethren, could

not speak to you as to spiritual men, but as to men of flesh, as to babes in Christ."

A baby is self-centered by nature. As cute as babies are, they are still self-centered. The only time we hear from them is when they have a need. One end or the other has a need.

There really is no problem with a baby being a baby. Babies are supposed to be self-centered. We want them to be the way they are. When we first meet Christ, we are much more taken up with our salvation than we are with our Savior. It's evident that this does not bother Christ any more than a parent is bothered by an infant's self-centeredness. When I was first saved it seemed every time I prayed I got an answer right away. It was almost as though everything I asked for was granted. Babies are basically given everything they want (within reason) because we understand that they cannot make it on their own. A baby being a baby is not the problem. Adults being babies is the problem.

The writer of Hebrews expressed this:

> For though by this time you ought to be teachers, you have need again for someone to teach you the elementary principles of the oracles of God, and you have come to need milk and not solid food (Heb. 5:12).

The bride was still in the very juvenile place of being more taken up with what it means to be a "King's Kid" than anything else. It's not that Jesus does not want to meet our needs — it's that He wants us to be interested in Him more than anything else. I believe the Church has brought this problem of immaturity on itself by emphasizing the benefits of the resurrection rather than the lordship of Christ.

We have drawn people to the Lord based on what will

be theirs as a result. The benefits of the Resurrection such as health, wealth, and prosperity have been the primary focuses of many churches. It's not that Jesus does not want us to live in those benefits, it's that He wants us to mature and become taken up with Him rather than things.

What would happen if churches emphasized the lordship of Christ and conforming to His image? We would possibly stop growing at a rapid rate. I have a pastor friend who was going through that very issue while I was ministering in his church. He shared with me how Jesus was impressing him to stop producing church services that simply tickled people's ears without bringing them to any point of consecration. Once he changed his approach, several people left the church, including family members and board members. We love things. We love the Christian life because of what we can gain from it. However, when it comes to redirecting our attention to the Son of God alone, we are just not interested. Immaturity!

POSITION TWO

After the bride had gone through certain events, causing her to see the process of abandonment, she stated her second position:

> "I am my beloved's and my beloved is mine,
> He who pastures {his flock} among the lilies"
> (Song of Sol. 6:3).

Some progress is evident here. She had herself before Him but now she mentions Him before herself. She said, "I am His." However, she then tagged on the end of her statement, "And He is mine." It is important for each of us to realize that abandonment is a process. It is not a simple thing to lay down your life.

As we grow in faith, we take more of what we consider bold steps. In reality we are still taking baby steps.

When a baby is learning how to walk, it often grasps the fingers of mom or dad as it wobbles along. The baby may consider itself quite adventurous by taking these tiny steps but true adventure or faith will come when it releases mom and dad's fingers.

The final part of her statement, "And He is mine," is a "holding on." It's like saying to the Lord, *"I am giving you this entire problem* (I am His). *I wash my hands of any involvement. You handle this, Lord. The only thing I will do is worry about it* (He is mine)." That would be like saying, *"Just in case you do not take care of it as you should, I will have worry, and that should help quite a bit."*

Part of the reason we struggle with abandoning ourselves unto God is that we have developed a society that does not need God. Actually, we do need God. It's just that with all the benefits available to us today we lean upon things more than the Lord himself.

I was once in Uganda, Africa, teaching a pastor's school. We had been out in the bush for a few days holding meetings in a remote village. After the school finished, we were driving along the highway back to the city of Kampala when we came upon a terrible accident. A small van ran head-on into a large truck. As we approached the accident scene, we saw that there were many people standing around. The accident victims (four people died) were still lying out in the open on the road completely uncovered.

As we slowly drove by, I said to our African host, "This must have just happened, there is not even an ambulance here yet."

Our host looked at me and said, "In Uganda there is no such thing. We do not have ambulances, nor do we have 911 as you have. These accident victims are on their own." I could not believe what he said.

I asked, "Then how will they get to the hospital?"

He said, "Someone will most likely take them in their

own car. They are completely at the mercy of the bystanders."

Most of the world lives without health insurance or any of the benefits we take for granted in America. One reason miracles are much more prevalent in Third World countries is because of what they depend upon. When we hold our crusades in Africa, we witness many miracles. But why shouldn't we? God is all these people have. We do not see many miracles in our country, but then again we do not need to — we have insurance.

When my wife and I started Pray-Tell Ministries, we had very little money so we decided to make certain concessions. One of those was that of going without health insurance. I considered this a step of faith. In reality, there was very little true faith involved, at least initially.

I had become so dependant upon insurance that I never really gave much thought to what would happen if I ever needed medical help. I did not need God; I had insurance. However, with time, and God proving himself faithful repeatedly, my faith level began to change. Since the beginning of this ministry in 1981, we have gone without health insurance. Today my perspective concerning this has changed so much that I would honestly be afraid to go back to putting my trust in man's system.

It was hard to let go of the fingers of health insurance. I had become so accustomed to holding on to insurance that to let go was quite difficult. Once I let go, I quickly grabbed onto the fingers of God. I was praying harder than ever. I had removed myself from man's system; I needed God. However, there was still a "hanging on" in my life. It was called "praying out of fear." I was afraid not to pray. What if something happened! I was going through the process of abandonment but had not arrived by any means.

I eventually came to the place called "peace of mind." Today I rarely even give any thought to the situation. I do not need to. I simply know that God will care for my family and me. He is not dependent upon my prayers. He is dependent upon my faith. Faith is the ability to let go of (die to) all the safeguards we have become dependent upon, knowing that God will care for us.

POSITION THREE

In the first few verses of the seventh chapter of the "Song" Solomon holds nothing back in expressing his obsession with the bride. She finally comes to an understanding of his love for her. She states it in Song of Solomon 7:10:

> "I am my beloved's, And his desire is for me."

This is her third and final "statement of position." Taylor says, "Notice that there is a complete reversal of positions in the progression of these testimonies. In her first confession, she serves the Lord for her own benefit. In effect, she said that she loved the Lord because He gave her the things that she wanted. In her final testimony, she could say, 'I am my beloved's.' Now he has become the center of her life. Instead of possessing the Lord, she is possessed by Him."[1]

She could come to this final position because she came into an understanding that His desire was toward her. This understanding is what allowed her to abandon herself unto Him. What is it to understand this? It's a full revelation of His love for us. When we understand that God's desire is toward us, we understand that His desire to meet every need in our life is great. It is even greater than our own desire is to meet the needs of our own children.

King David came to this understanding when he said:

> I have been young, and now I am old; Yet I have not seen the righteous forsaken, Or his descendants begging bread (Ps. 37:25).

It took David many years to understand this. However, he eventually grasped the fact that God's desire was toward him. He no longer had to try to control his life because His God's desire was toward him. He could lay the control of his life down knowing that it was completely safe in the hands of a loving God.

ONLY ONE LOVE

"The king has brought me into his chambers" (Song of Sol. 1:4).

The "chambers" is literally the bedroom. Throughout this book we see the King's desire to bring the bride to a place of intimacy. However, there is a problem. She has more than one love. Initially she loves herself more than she loves him. As long as there are other loves, she does not qualify to be brought into the chambers.

Did you know that Jesus does not want to be number one on your list? *He wants to be your entire list!* He is not impressed with being the best of your many loves. Imagine my wife's surprise if I announced to her one day that I currently loved many different women but that I loved her more than any of the others. Then I assured her that I had her on the top of my list. How impressed would she be with that? She does not want to be number one on my list of loves. She wants to be my list. As my wife, she has every right to expect that. Somehow, we have come to believe that if we keep Jesus at the top of our "list of many loves," He will still be pleased with us. Not so!

It is not uncommon to find that the intimacy of a relationship is damaged greatly upon the revelation of another love. If a wife finds out that her husband loves another woman, it is not uncommon for her to say something like this: "If you have her, you will not have me." There is no more intimacy until the other love is done away with completely.

THE HARLOT SPIRIT

Having other loves is referred to by God as the "spirit of harlotry." The harlot spirit can be a confusing one. It is never satisfied with only one love. It can profess love for anything, but it cannot be satisfied with only one love. Pastors see this all the time in their churches. They spiritually discern that something is missing in the life of one of their people. Upon questioning them they ask, "Do you really love God?" The individual with the harlot spirit can easily respond by saying, "Of course I love God," and mean it. The problem is that they cannot love just God. They must have their other loves also.

Hosea the prophet was trying to bring this message to the people of his day. Hosea was asked to marry the prostitute Gomer.

> Go, take to yourself a wife of harlotry, and {have} children of harlotry; for the land commits flagrant harlotry, forsaking the LORD (Hos. 1:2–3).

Hosea obeyed God and married Gomer. Gomer eventually left him. Hosea then became a living example to the people of Israel about what they had done to God. Hosea is a type of God the Father, while Gomer is a type of Israel. Because Israel had so many different loves, she really could not draw close to God.

> Their deeds will not allow them To return to their God. For a spirit of harlotry is within them, And they do not know the LORD (Hos. 5:4).

Because of a spirit of harlotry, they could not know the Lord. This explains some of the trouble we have in drawing close to the Lord. Most Christians want to pray much more than they do. However, many find that for some reason they simply cannot develop the intimacy they want with the Lord. This verse simply tells us that we cannot know the Lord while a spirit of harlotry exists within us. We must abandon all other loves. Then and only then are we able to enter the chambers with Him.

INSECURITY

It's a historical fact that whenever the church stops praying, she becomes a militant church. There is a reason for this. We are seeking security. God made the woman with a need for security. Ideally, a woman will draw her security from her husband's relationship with Christ. If a woman is married to a man who does not seek God, then she seeks to control the home. She does not do this out of some great desire to take over the leadership of her home. She is simply feeding her need for security. If her husband is not committed to God, she has a problem laying her life in his hands.

How easy would it be for us to lay our lives in the hands of Christ if he were not fully committed to His Father? Suppose Jesus had spoken to this effect while He was on earth: "When it comes to the Father, I can take Him or leave Him," or "I usually obey Him." Our salvation was dependent upon our Lord's complete commitment to His Father. It would be very difficult to simply lay our lives in His hands if we felt He might not obey God. We would probably try to earn our salvation rather than leaving it in the hands of someone not fully committed.

When the Church (the Bride) stops spending time in prayer, she lacks intimacy with Christ. From the lack of intimacy she feels insecure. Therefore, she develops a militant attitude. The church's current militant attitude comes from the lack of intimacy with Christ. We are striving to control society today. We are attempting to establish a certain lifestyle that is free of crime, greed, and injustice. All of those things are fine. I believe that is exactly how the

Lord would have us live. Our problems come from an inability to believe that Jesus can actually handle the world.

The lack of a deep prayer life is from having more
than one love in our lives. Because of these other loves, we
cannot be brought into the chambers. Therefore, our intimacy with Him never fully develops. Subsequently, we remain insecure. We know we should surrender, but we
struggle with it. Our option is simple. Give up the other
gods! There is to be only one love in our life, and it must
be Jesus. As you make Him your one and only love, you
will find yourself being escorted into the chambers by the
Lord himself.

CHAPTER NINE

THE SPOTLESS BRIDE

"You are altogether beautiful, my darling,
And there is no blemish in you" (Song of Sol. 4:7).

This was part of the conversation Solomon and the
bride were having in his secret place. Solomon in-
vested a considerable amount of time in the development of his bride. Getting her to climb the steep pathway was no small task. He even left his place of royalty to
come to where she was to help her become what she needed
to be. He wanted a beautiful bride.

Abishag was very beautiful outwardly. This is why
she was originally picked to serve King David (see 1 Kings
1:3). Solomon was working on her inner beauty. He was
working on her spirit. He understood the beauty of self-
lessness. He understood the beauty of humility and lowliness. He himself displayed his own lowliness in his willingness to leave his place of glory to come and work in the
vineyard. He understood that there is no blemish in holiness. The bride really could not be without spot or wrinkle
until she gave up her love of self and completely abandoned herself unto him.

This is very similar to what Paul wrote about how Jesus came to prepare His bride:

> [So] that He might sanctify her, having cleansed her by the washing of water with the word, that He might present to Himself the church in all her glory, having no spot or wrinkle or any such thing; but that she would be holy and blameless (Eph. 5:26–27).

Jesus wants a beautiful, spotless bride. He wants a bride that is holy and blameless. Therefore, He spends all of His time preparing her for her wedding day. However, a bride is not made beautiful by focusing on herself, but by focusing on her groom.

The bride of Christ (the Church) today has a serious problem called self-centeredness. She focuses much more on her own external beauty than she does her Lord. In the Book of 1 Samuel we see something very similar. Hannah's husband was addressing this issue after he noticed that Hannah was far more interested in having a child than she was in him.

> Then Elkanah her husband said to her, "Hannah, why do you weep and why do you not eat and why is your heart sad? Am I not better to you than ten sons? (1 Sam. 1:8).

Hannah was absorbed with having a son. This is relatively natural. It is not unusual for a woman to want to bear a child. However, after some time of weeping and wailing, Elkanah spoke to his wife. He said in essence, "Why are you so taken up with having a child when you already have me? "Am I not better than ten sons?"

The average woman's response to this today would be something like, "Who does he think he is?" That is a good question. Who did Elkanah think he was? I would imagine he thought he was her husband. He probably also thought he was her protector and provider. More important than all of that, the husband is the one who represents Christ in the home.

Elkanah lived in a day where it was not unusual for a man to have more than one wife. The following verses reveal this:

> He had two wives: the name of one was Hannah and the name of the other Peninnah; and Peninnah had children, but Hannah had no children. . . . When the day came that Elkanah sacrificed, he would give portions to Peninnah his wife and to all her sons and her daughters; but to Hannah he would give a double portion, for he loved Hannah, but the LORD had closed her womb (1 Sam. 1:2–5).

Because Hannah had no children, she made the common mistake of believing that she could please her husband by giving him a child. Elkanah was trying to tell her that he was content with simply having her. He even gave her a double portion to prove his love for her. Elkanah would have loved a child by her. But he was trying to make an equally important point. He wanted her to understand that her relationship with him was the primary source of his happiness.

Consider how society views the husband. Today he is the scum. Many women have very little respect for their husbands. Hollywood depicts him as a goof-off that cannot understand the basics of life. If a man said to his wife, "Am I not better to you than ten sons?" he would be laughed to death.

The disdain that we see for the husband today comes from the Church's perspective of Christ. Husbands and wives represent Christ and the Church. Therefore, society becomes a reflection of the relationship Christ has with His Bride. The moral climate of society typically reflects the spiritual condition of the Church. Suppose Jesus were to say to the average family in our churches today, "You have me, am I not better than a large family?" How would a statement like that be received?

Our church families today are not infatuated with Jesus; they are infatuated with themselves.

FAMILY WORSHIP

There is an interesting phenomenon going on today in the Church. There is a worship of family over God. Young couple after young couple no longer go to church Sunday night because they need a "family night." I believe "family night" is important also, but why not have it Friday night or Saturday night rather than Sunday night? The average response to that question is, "Friday and Saturday nights are used for other things." So what we have decided to do is use Sunday night to focus in on ourselves instead of God.

Because of a lack of participation, many churches have been forced to cancel their Sunday night services. This lack of respect for God and the subsequent worship of family is a mirror of the Church's lack of prayer and the exaltation of itself.

Some would argue that you don't need to go to church a lot to be a Christian. I suppose that is true. However, if you are a Christian why would you not want to go to church a lot? The issue is not really a matter of going to church, it's a matter of desire. The reason Sunday nights became a church night was from people wanting to be in the presence of God.

In the midst of revival, believers would approach their pastors with a desire to come back to church in the evening. They wanted the presence of God. They were not going to church from some legalistic motive. They desired to be with God. Therefore, the lack of desire to come back on Sunday evening stems from spiritual decline. The tragedy is not that people are not going to church on Sunday nights. The tragedy is that they do not *want* to go back.

When prayer is a priority in the church, it is the same as the wife saying that her husband means more to her than anything else. When the church fails to keep prayer first, she is in essence rejecting Christ's authoritative role in her life. This is then reflected in the wife's attitude toward her husband. Her whole attention then goes to developing her own home (family). If a pastor is not a person of prayer, his whole attention goes toward developing the size of his church.

THE HEART OF THE BRIDE

"My mother's sons were angry with me;
They made me caretaker of the vineyards, {But}
I have not taken care of my own vineyard" (Song
of Sol. 1:6).

We notice again a significant difference between the bride and the daughters of Zion here. The daughters of Zion, the watchmen, or the friends of the bride, are those who are a part of the family of God but lack intimacy with God. They focus more on the work of God while the bride focuses on the God of the work.

Abishag's brothers were upset with her because she had been sent back to her home after having served King David. They liked all the prestige they received. They enjoyed having a sister in the service of the king. When King David died and Abishag was sent home, their plans for greatness died also. To punish her, they put her to work in the fields. They gave her the menial task of tending the vineyard.

We can see the heart of the bride in the preceding

verse. Abishag had the type of heart that could be drawn; some do not. She was not so much complaining that she had to work in the vineyard, it's that she felt her priorities were out of order. She says in essence, "Here I am working this vineyard while my own vineyard is unattended." Abishag understood the hypocrisy of trying to do something effectively while her own life was not in order. The daughters just don't get it. They never seem to understand that the work of God cannot be accomplished to its fullest extent without a pre-eminent focus on the God of the work.

This reveals to us a little about the heart of the bride. The bride understands introspection. The bride is drawn to intimacy. The bride longs for self-cleansing. The daughters of Zion, on the other hand, understand very little of the importance of these things. They serve God from a distance. They are busy about His work, but have no real longing just for Him.

MY HOUSE LIES DESOLATE!

In the Book of Haggai, God is calling upon the people to rebuild His temple. He draws an analogy between the house of God and their own houses.

> Is it time for you yourselves to dwell in your paneled houses while this house {lies} desolate? (Hag. 1:4).

A paneled house would represent a very elegant home. The foundation of the temple had been laid 14 years before. Considerable progress had been made in the building itself, but for some time it had been lying in an unfinished state. God challenged them and said in essence, "Why are you putting all of your time and money into your own homes while mine goes unfinished?"

> Now therefore, thus says the LORD of hosts, "Consider your ways!" (Hag. 1:5).

Consider what is happening to you! God says in essence, "Can't you read the writing on the wall?"

> You have sown much, but harvest little; {you} eat, but {there is} not {enough} to be satisfied; {you} drink, but {there is} not {enough} to become drunk; {you} put on clothing, but no one is warm {enough}; and he who earns, earns wages {to put} into a purse with holes (Hag. 1:6).

There is never enough. You work hard but gain very little. Why is this? Verse seven gives us the answer:

> Thus says the LORD of hosts, "Consider your ways!" (Hag. 1:7).

The reason life is the way it is, is because we tend to put the development of our families before God. Many families that are putting themselves before their worship of God are finding that in the end they lose their children spiritually. Yet "family night" was something they were doing for the spiritual sake of their children. We can build fine families. However, if we put our families before God, all we will end up with is a fine family, not a spiritual family.

Why is it we are concerned with our own houses while the house of God is neglected? I believe the whole issue is pride. I was teaching in a Sunday school class once when a mom asked an interesting question. I had been talking about pride and our struggle with it when she said, "Is it wrong to be proud of our own children?" She continued, "I'm very proud of my three boys. I try to encourage them so that they will be successful in life."

I said to her, "Why not just love your boys? What would be wrong with that? Loving them would be more significant than being proud of them." On different occasions God spoke concerning His Son in a voice that could be heard by those around Him and He said, "This is my

Son in whom I am pleased." Why not just say that we are pleased with our children rather than being proud of them.

Here is what happens when we are proud of our children. Pride exalts them. Taking pride in our children is that of putting them before God. Subsequently, we put their success before their spirituality, all in the name of Christianity. We will support them in their worldly pursuits while simultaneously they go downhill spiritually. Soon school events replace church events. That simply translates into an adult life that allows a person's work to come before his worship of God. Yet he believes he is pleasing God. Many pastors will put their church's success before its spirituality. They are proud of their achievements in the community, and yet you could not find the presence of God there if you had to.

When you love something rather than simply taking pride in something, you will do whatever you must to make it a spiritual success. When you truly love someone, you want God's best for him or her. Relationship with God then means more than anything else. Success is not the problem. It is possible to be successful and spiritual, but rare. When you love, you will see to it that Jesus comes first. This is what the bride meant when she said that she was being forced to care for other vineyards while her own was unattended. She understood that her relationship with Christ was to come first, then she could more effectively work the vineyard of others.

I do not take pride in my son. I love my son. How can I take pride in something that I had nothing to do with? I did not create him or design him. I did not give him his personality. When you take pride in your children, you are taking credit for something you had nothing to do with. It's an exaltation of self and them. When Jesus is first, we love. When we are first, we become proud. If we are proud we will build our own house while the house of God sits in ruin.

"{You} look for much, but behold, {it comes} to little; when you bring {it} home, I blow it {away}." Haggai 1:9 tells us that all of our efforts are nothing more than boxing the wind. If we give ourselves to the development of our families before we honor the Lord, we end up with emptiness. The last part of verse nine explains:

"Why?" declares the LORD of hosts, "Because of My house which {lies} desolate, while each of you runs to his own house" (Hag. 1:9).

A person may say, "Is not family something God supports?" Certainly, family is God's idea. However, God's idea of family is to put Him first. How can we develop a healthy family if we do not teach our kids that the worship of God is our primary purpose?

Our families are reflecting the Church's priorities. The lack of prayer in the Church suggests the worship of itself over God. The Church is like Hannah. We weep over our size and prestige while Jesus says to us, "But you have me, am I not better?" We say, "But doesn't Jesus want us to reach people?" Certainly He does. "Doesn't Jesus want our churches to grow?" Certainly, but he wants it to grow through intimacy with Him not through an infatuation with itself.

Jesus is all for the family. However, He wants families to grow through him. Do you think He is excited about a focus on the family to the exclusion of himself?

MARRIED TO JESUS OR SELF?

There are basically two types of believers. There are those who are married to Jesus, and there are those who are married to the Church. The bride in the "Song" was taken up with the groom. The daughters were taken up with the vineyard. I was once doing a three-day meeting for Rev. Paul Martin in Washington, Illinois. We were sitting in his office talking about the church as an organization. In the midst of our conversation, Paul turned to me and said, "Brother, I am not married to the Church, I am married to Jesus." From that time on, I began to see a difference in believers. Some are obsessed with their church. Others are obsessed with their Savior. Here again we see a difference between the bride and the daughters. The bride is taken up with the groom while the daughters are taken up with themselves.

The bride finally responded to the wooing of the groom in chapter 5 of the "Song" and opened the door. However, she found that her lover had already departed because of her hesitation. Subsequently, she went on a search for him:

> "I opened for my lover, but my lover had left; he was gone. My heart sank at his departure. I looked for him but did not find him. I called him but he did not answer. The watchmen found me as they made their rounds in the city. They beat me, they bruised me; they took away my cloak, those watchmen of the walls! O daughters of Jerusalem, I charge you — if you find my lover, what will you tell him? Tell him I am faint with love.
>
> "How is your beloved better than others, most beautiful of women? How is your beloved better than others, that you charge us so?" (Song of Sol. 5:6–9;NIV).

As the bride goes on a search for her lover, she meets the watchmen. Although they beat and bruised her, the watchmen are not technically bad people. They are simply people who cannot understand intimacy. The bride is obsessed with her love while the watchmen (daughters) are obsessed with themselves.

In verse nine we see their hearts when they say in essence, "Why is your love better than our love?" I run into this all the time in my prayer seminars. I am trying to cause the Church to see her need to be taken up with Jesus and yet she cannot see beyond herself. They will "Amen" my teaching about prayer because they see how it can benefit them. Their prayer life is focused around what they can get from God.

When the bride says in essence, "My lover is the most important thing there is," the watchmen beat her and bruise her with their derogatory remarks. They do not understand her intimacy. They believe that what they are doing (building the church/families) is just as important, thus they say, "How is your beloved better than ours?"

When I was saved, I lived in a house with some other guys. These other guys were not Christians. Whenever they would use the name of the Lord in vain, it was like taking a knife and sticking it in my heart. Every derogatory remark about my newly found love bruised me.

MINISTERING TO GOD

In the Book of Ezekiel we see two different types of priests.

> But the Levites who went far from Me, when Israel went astray, who went astray from Me after their idols, shall bear the punishment for their iniquity. Yet they shall be ministers in My sanctuary, having oversight at the gates of the house and ministering in the house; they shall slaughter the burnt offering and the sacrifice for the people, and they shall stand before them to minister to them (Ezek. 44:10–11).

First we see a group of priests who were more interested in themselves than they were God. When Israel went

after idols, these priests allowed them to bring them into
the house of God. They allowed them to use idols as part
of their worship. These priests are much more taken up
with the church and its status in the community than anything else. Verse 11 tells us they are the overseers (watchmen) of the house of God.

I find it quite interesting that they could remain as
ministers. They may continue to go about the work of God.
However, they are not able to minister to the God of the
work.

> And they shall not come near to Me to serve
> as a priest to Me, nor come near to any of My
> holy things, to the things that are most holy; but
> they shall bear their shame and their abomina-
> tions which they have committed (Ezek. 44:13).

Because they did not understand intimacy, they did
not understand holiness. Holiness is separation. There must
be separation before intimacy. They allowed Israel to bring
the world into the temple. Subsequently, they are no longer
able to come near God's holy things. They have come to
the place where they cannot discern between the holy and
the profane.

The watchmen are fully convinced that what they are
doing (serving God) is just as important as seeking God.
Therefore, they say to the bride, "Why is your love better
than our love?"

There is yet another group of priests. — the sons of
Zadok. We read of them in the following verses.

> "But the Levitical priests, the sons of
> Zadok, who kept charge of My sanctuary when
> the sons of Israel went astray from Me, shall
> come near to Me to minister to Me; and they
> shall stand before Me to offer Me the fat and the
> blood," declares the Lord GOD. "They shall en-

ter My sanctuary; they shall come near to My
table to minister to Me and keep My charge"
(Ezek. 44:15–16).

These priests represent the heart of the bride. They
are not as taken up with the work of God as they are with
the God of the work. When Israel goes into idolatry, the
sons of Zadok maintain the high standard of holiness and
do not allow them to bring it into the sanctuary. Subsequently, they are the ones who can minister to God himself.

They understand separation. They understand that
there is no intimacy without separation. Because of their
infatuation with the Lord himself, they will not allow anything in the sanctuary that does not glorify Him.

Moreover, they shall teach My people {the
difference} between the holy and the profane, and
cause them to discern between the unclean and
the clean (Ezek. 44:23).

The only way to understand the difference between
the holy and the profane is through the separation that
comes through intimacy. The bride understands this; the
watchmen do not. The daughters of Zion are in love with
themselves. They are in love with the work. They will do
anything to make the work look good, even if it means
compromise. The daughters believe the end justifies the
means.

There are many pastors who are much more like the
daughters than the bride. Subsequently, they are not able
to teach the difference between the holy and the profane,
or common. This is why there is such a lack of discernment concerning holiness today. The Church is not being
taught by the example of its pastors. If a pastor does want
to take a stand and uphold God's holy standards, he is
classified as legalistic.

MARRIED TO SELF

Can you be married to yourself? NO! Yet that is exactly what we are when we are taken up with ourselves rather than Jesus. The Church is the Bride, but if the Church is not obsessed with Jesus, then she is obsessed with herself. Worshiping our families over God is very much like a church that puts itself before God. Self-centeredness is a false love.

There is no need for us to be obsessed with ourselves because Jesus is. From His perspective this is all about us, His bride. He wants to possess His bride. He gave His life for His bride. He will do and give anything for His bride.

Our perspective is to be Him. Our life is to be all about Him, not us. We are to give our lives to Him. We are to interest ourselves with His needs and His concerns.

THE BEAUTY OF SURRENDER

Have you ever seen anything more beautiful than a bride? There is something about a bride that is very attractive, but what is it? Is it her gown? Is it her makeup? Is it her shoes? No, her beauty is her self-lessness.

They looked to Him and were radiant (Ps. 34:5).

Those who give themselves to the Lord develop a radiance about themselves. The radiance of the bride is her willingness to give herself to her groom. That which attracts a man to a woman is her willingness to give herself over. Her radiance comes out of her desire to surrender intimately to her groom.

When the bride longs for the king, she is most beautiful. However, if a bride is in love with herself and infatuated with her own beauty, she is no longer attractive. Outwardly speaking, she may be the most beautiful woman in the world getting ready to be married. However, if she is more in love with herself than her groom, there is no longer an attraction. There will be nothing left to draw the hearts of men. Men are drawn to surrender.

Suppose the guests are awaiting the entrance of the bride for the wedding ceremony when suddenly the back doors open, and there she stands. Everyone rises in her honor. Upon seeing everybody look at her, she realizes her own outward beauty so she stops and strikes a few poses for a while so everybody can soak in her beauty. At that point all the men in the audience would think to themselves, *That poor groom. His bride is more in love with herself than she is with him.* Gone would be her beauty. When the Church's beauty becomes the thing she focuses in on, something is out of order. She, in effect, then focuses on building her own kingdom.

PROPHET OR KING?

Hannah eventually gave birth to Samuel. Samuel became a great prophet. He was the last prophet to judge Israel as its leader. When Samuel's rule came to an end, Israel demanded a king to rule over them.

Why did Israel want a king instead of a prophet? It's because Israel was more taken up with herself than her God. A king wants a kingdom. A king will do anything for the sake of the kingdom. The prophet wants God. He will do anything for God's sake.

When the Church is taken up with itself, it tends to reject the voice of the prophet. It begins to exalt its pastors like kings. Israel wanting a king is similar to a church being content with ministers who do not pray. Ministers that pray maintain a prophetic voice. The prophet will not let us get away from God. The king will. The king is interested in his kingdom. The prophet's voice gets in his way.

The prophet will come on the scene and point out all the ways the Church is worshiping itself. The king will glory in the Church worshiping itself for that exalts him.

When the Church stopped praying, she went away from the prophetic voice of Jesus. Being removed from His voice and influence, she began to exalt herself. The lack of prayer is always because of the worship of self over God. Subsequently, she became quite self-centered, no longer able to discern between the holy and the profane.

Our families began to reflect the priorities of the Church. We became infatuated with ourselves. We now worship ourselves over our God. Subsequently, we cannot discern between the holy and the profane. We allow the world to come into our homes. We may still be involved in the work of God, but we are not allowed to minister to Him.

The problem with all of this is that from the lack of discernment, the Church really does not care about its current condition. If you challenge the Church to abandon its love of self and to go after the Lord, its response is, "Why is your love better than our love?"

CHAPTER TEN

COME, MY BELOVED!

"I am my beloved's, And his desire is for me. Come, my beloved, let us go out into the country, Let us spend the night in the villages. Let us rise early {and go} to the vineyards; Let us see whether the vine has budded {And its} blossoms have opened, {And whether} the pomegranates have bloomed. There I will give you my love" (Song of Sol. 7:10–12).

These are the words of the bride. First she expresses her total commitment to him stating, "I am my beloved's," then she asks him to join her intimately. The power of the bride's words comes from her surrender to the groom. Typically, men are initiators and women are responders. If a man initiates intimacy, but there is no response from the woman, then there is no intimacy. I am talking in a general sense. Obviously, there are times between husband and wife when these roles are reversed. However, it is much more typical for the man to be the pursuer than the woman.

Any man who is a pursuer would consider it a very special event when his wife initiates intimacy instead of himself. In our opening verses, the bride is doing just that. She is saying, "Come my beloved . . . let's spend the night together . . . and there I will give you my love." What more could a groom ask for than to have a bride who wants him?

The reason this would be so thrilling to the groom is that his bride is expressing that she wants to be drawn close to him. Consider this — in most marriages the woman controls the intimacy, not the man. I am referring to a marriage that is in order. In today's society we need to be careful whenever we use the family as an analogy of the Church. There is so much out of order in our homes today that it is difficult for everyone to identify with this. However, in a marriage that is in order, where the man is not using force or manipulation, the woman controls the level of intimacy.

We see a great example of this in Christ's relationship with His bride the Church. The Church can get just as close to Jesus as she wants. Whenever the Church desires, she can pray and draw as near to Jesus as she prefers. Jesus will never turn down any spiritual advance of His Bride. He is very much in the male role here. So the Church can get as close to Jesus as she wants. However, Jesus can only get as close to the Church as she allows. It does not matter how much Jesus wants to be with His Church. It does not matter how often He initiates prayer. If she will not respond there is no prayer; hence, no intimacy.

This is not something the Church should develop a haughty spirit about and view as something she has over Christ. The Church is to live in submission to Christ. Submission develops humility. Humility is placing yourself under someone else. It is honestly seeing others as "better" than yourself. Therefore, revival becomes that of the Bride allowing Christ the intimacy He desires. Revival is the Bride giving herself over to the wooing of Christ. In the Church's case, it is her responding to the call to prayer

and repentance. Intimacy always means renewal and revival of any relationship. The life of any relationship is
found in intimacy.

There is another facet of this that makes it quite special. Initially, the bride sought the groom for what she could
gain from Him. Now she is saying that she is simply taken
up with Him rather than with the things she can gain from
Him. This is expressed when she says, "Let us spend the
night in the villages, and then rise early to go to the vineyard where the vine has budded and the pomegranates have
bloomed."

I like what Matthew Henry says concerning this:

> She is willing to rise betimes, to go along
> with her beloved: Let us get up early to the vine-
> yards. It intimates her care to improve opportu-
> nities of conversing with her beloved; Those that
> will go abroad with Christ must begin betimes
> with him, early in the morning of their days, must
> begin every day with him, seek him early, seek
> him diligently. She will be content to take up her
> lodging in the villages, the huts or cottages which
> the country people built for their shelter when
> they attended their business in the fields; there,
> in these mean and cold dwellings, she will gladly
> reside, if she may but have her beloved with her.
> His presence will make them fine and pleasant,
> and convert them into palaces. A gracious soul
> can reconcile itself to the poorest accommoda-
> tions, if it may have communion with God in
> them. The most pleasant delightful fields, even
> in the springtime, when the country is most pleas-
> ant, will not satisfy her, unless she has her be-
> loved with her. No delights on earth can make a
> believer easy, unless he enjoys God in all.[1]

GROWING THE VINEYARD

I find it quite interesting that the bride wants to go to the vineyard. The vineyard represents the work of God. One difference between the bride and the daughters is that the bride's interest in the vineyard comes through her desire to please the groom. In other words, she has a priority of putting her relationship with the Lord before the work of the Lord. The daughters have different priorities. They put the work of the Lord before the Lord of the work.

The primary problem with the daughters was not their interest in the vineyard (the work of God) but the priorities of their life. They felt that tending the vineyard was all that was necessary to please their master. Not so! The focus and drive to tend the vineyard is to come from a great longing to do whatever it takes to draw close to the master. As important as the vineyard is, the work of God is to be a by-product of our passion for Jesus Himself.

Without the vineyard being cared for, the kingdom of God does not grow. Until a person understands intimacy, this will always remain confusing. I teach on the subject of prayer from the perspective of it being communion with God, worshiping God, thanking God, and meditating on Him. This usually causes many people to say, "But if I do not address my needs or the needs of others, nothing will get done." "How can we tend the vineyard without focusing on the specific things that need to be addressed?" they question.

It is as difficult to answer that as it was for the daughters to grasp what was going on between the groom and the bride in the "Song." They could not see the value of just being with him.

What is it that cannot be accomplished through His presence? We often say, "God is the answer," and yet we seek answers rather than God. The daughters seek answers from God while the bride seeks God as the answer. When

I was a child, I needed my parents more than I needed anything else. Whenever I would hurt myself by falling or getting hit by something, I would come into the house crying. What I needed then was my mom. I needed her to be there. I needed her to put her arms around me. I also needed her to kiss it and make it better. I needed my mom more than I needed a Band-Aid.

Somehow the Church today has forgotten her need for the Lord himself and simply seeks the Band-Aid. When we pray, we typically ask God to make it better through the Band-Aid rather than through His presence. Suppose we got our healing but failed to draw close to God. Would a healing without a closeness to the Lord be all that we need? Suppose we got our financial "miracle" but failed to draw close to the Lord through it? Is money what we need the most? Suppose God heals our marriages but we are not drawn closer to the Lord through it. Do our marriages now have all they need to stay together?

Though God wants our needs met (He wants to apply the Band-Aid), He wants them met in a way that will draw us close to Him. He wants to apply the Band-Aid while He nurtures us. The bride can accomplish the work of God in a way that nurtures. The daughters cannot. They lack the kind of intimacy with Him that will allow them to develop the ability to nurture. Therefore, they teach people to seek answers rather than God. They do not have anything to offer people but answers.

TRAVAIL

My children, with whom I am again in labor until Christ is formed in you — (Gal. 4:19).

The apostle Paul here is referring to himself as the bride of Christ, travailing in prayer, until Christ is formed in the heart of someone. The way the vineyard grows is through birth. People must be born (again) into the Kingdom, but birthing requires intimacy. A couple can desire to give birth to a child all they want, but without intimacy there is only a desire. This is where much of the Church is today. We want revival but lack the intimacy needed to birth it.

There are those today who are teaching that the Church needs to travail in prayer until she gives birth. The problem with this teaching is that it emphasizes travailing rather than that which leads to travailing. A woman cannot, on her own, bring herself to a place of travailing. Travailing is the result of intimacy. I have met women who will even get into the fetal position while they pray so as to make a statement of birth to the Lord. This is all pointless. We do not travail through any decision or action of ours.

Travailing in prayer is the end result of a burden growing within us that ultimately brings us to a place where we must "pray it through." That burden is placed there by the Lord himself as we commune with Him in prayer. It is possible to be brought to a place in prayer described in the Book of Romans as, "groanings too deep for words."

A pregnant woman does not decide when she will give birth. She will give birth when the seed within her comes to maturity and not before. She cannot decide to simply travail when she wants to. However, when it is time to travail, she cannot stop it, either. The point is, travailing is a result of intimacy. Our focus should be on that and nothing else.

It's interesting to note that birthing depends on the bride, not the groom. In this light we see that Christ cannot give birth to revival because it is not His role. Christ seeks to draw His Bride into intimacy (the secret place) with Him. Through that, she can be brought to a place of birthing. The daughter can tend the vineyard but cannot cause any spiritual growth because of the inability to give birth. She is more like the babysitter than anything else.

Birthing develops the ability to nurture. It is a pregnant woman that gains the ability to nurture at her breast. The ability to nurture is what draws people to the kingdom. The apostle Peter refers to this in 1 Peter 2:2:

> Like newborn babes, long for the pure milk of the word, that by it you may grow in respect to salvation.

Babies long for pure milk. It is an innate desire. Jesus said that no man can come to Him unless the Father draws him (see John 6:44). The Holy Spirit draws us toward our source of nurture. This is why you cannot have revival without prayer first. Prayer, or intimacy with Christ, is what gives the bride the ability to nurture. Revival without prayer would be like a 13-year-old girl having a baby. It's possible, but she is not ready for it in any way.

NOTHING TO OFFER

> "We have a little sister, And she has no breasts; What shall we do for our sister On the day when she is spoken for?" (Song of Sol. 8:8).

In this verse, a question is posed to the bride concerning one of the daughters. It will be important to understand here that the woman's breast in the "Song" is referred to as a nurturing agent more so than as a sexual item.

Nurturing is a drawing agent. The friends of the bride are beginning to realize that this young sister has very little about her that is a draw or an attraction to others. Since she lacks intimacy with the groom, she does not have the ability to nurture. Subsequently, she does not attract others to herself.

I started traveling full-time teaching on prayer in 1981. After a handful of years on the road, the pastor at my home church asked if I would consider becoming his minister of prayer. It was to be a one-year experiment to see what would happen if prayer had a priority in the church. I decided to do it on a part-time basis. I still traveled some weeks each month but primarily gave my time and efforts into the prayer ministry of our church.

Prayer was preached, it was taught, and it was practiced. We developed many different prayer thrusts throughout the year. Before this time, the church had been growing at a rate of less than 100 people a year. There is nothing wrong with a church growing at that rate. However, during the year we set aside to give prayer the priority of the church, our attendance increased by 400 people. We went from less than 100 new people a year to over 400 new people in one year.

The most common testimony of those that were getting saved each week (we averaged eight to ten salvations a week) was that they really did not know why they started coming to our church. They simply felt compelled to come. The Spirit of God was clearly drawing them because our church could nurture.

LIFE THROUGH DEATH

The kingdom of God works from a very simple principle: life comes through death. We have the spiritual life we have today because of the death of Christ. Our life comes through His death. Today, we who have the Spirit of Christ within us are being challenged to lay our lives down so that others can gain life. Laying our life down has to do with developing intimacy with Christ. It is a "giving over" to the will of Jesus.

Intercession is also a "laying down of your life." Intercession is something you do for the sake of others. You are, in effect, giving up your life so that the ones you are praying for can gain life. Laying down your life is a surrender. It is also the picture of intimacy. It is only through intimacy that a woman gains the ability to nurture. If there is no surrender of herself to her groom, she does not develop the ability to draw others.

The church that will come together and pray is collectively laying down its life for its community. Their death puts light and life into a dark world. As people begin to respond to the light, they are naturally drawn to its source. The "source" is the church that is praying, because that is the church that can nurture.

God will draw those that are new, or babes, to where they can be cared for. The church that does not pray is like the young sister that has no breasts. It has no appeal, no drawing. Nature teaches us this. A man, by nature, is attracted to the shape of a mature woman. What the "Song" is teaching us is that when the bride gives herself to the groom intimately, she becomes quite attractive to others.

In chapter 2 of the "Song," verse 14 has the groom revealing part of his nature. He says, "Let me see your form, Let me hear your voice; For your voice is sweet, And your form is lovely." The "form" of the bride ministers to the groom. This is not just a sexual issue, though it is very much a part of nature. Only through intimacy can the groom see the form of his bride. Her form however, represents her ability to nurture. The groom is just as interested in caring for his children as the bride. The groom also knows that he is limited in what he can offer his children. Therefore, when the bride's breasts are like "towers" (see Song of Sol. 8:10), he is ministered to because he knows she now can nurture. He can now rest in his relationship with her. She has followed him to the secret place. She has put him before her. Now the vineyard will be cared for properly.

SOMETHING TO OFFER

After the friends of the bride talk about the young sister who has nothing to offer, the bride makes a comment about herself.

"I am a wall, and my breasts are like towers. Thus I have become in his eyes like one bringing contentment" (Song of Sol. 8:10;NIV).

When she referred to her own breasts as towers, she
was saying in essence, "I can nurture. Subsequently, I can
bring contentment to my groom." The greatest difference
between the bride and the daughters is intimacy. The bride
gives herself over to intimacy, but the daughters do not.
The daughters cannot be taught the need for a prayer life.
The daughters may "amen" the message of prayer, but
never actually develop a pursuit of the groom.

The bride is most attractive because of her surrender.
She can draw/birth people into the kingdom through her
relationship with her groom. Subsequently her single motive in life, developing intimacy with her groom, is what
equips her to accomplish the work of God in a most effective way.

CHAPTER ELEVEN

FOOLISH OR WISE?

In this chapter we are going to continue to look at the difference between the daughters and the bride. In Matthew chapter 25 there is a great lesson that we need to heed.

As Jesus was teaching about being ready for His coming, He compared five wise virgins to five foolish virgins.

> Then the kingdom of heaven will be comparable to ten virgins, who took their lamps, and went out to meet the bridegroom. And five of them were foolish, and five were prudent. For when the foolish [heedless] took their lamps, they took no oil with them (Matt. 25:1–3).

Five were foolish. The word "foolish" means *heedless*. All of the virgins were instructed to live in a state of readiness, but the five foolish ones never heeded the message. However, the other five virgins were prudent. The word "prudent" means *wise* or *clear-eyed*. They took the message seriously.

> But the prudent took oil in flasks along with their lamps (Matt. 25:4).

When the bridegroom appeared the prudent were ready. The five wise virgins lived in a state of readiness and pursuit. When He appeared they saw Him with no shame, subsequently they went with Him. The foolish were heedless. They did not listen to the prompting of the Spirit. They did not develop a pursuit that purified them in the process. When He appeared, they were gone. They did not see Him because you can only see Him to the same degree you have developed in His character.

There is an interesting parallel here. The five wise virgins are similar in spirit to the bride in the "Song." The five foolish virgins are similar in spirit to the daughters of Zion in the "Song." Though the wise and the foolish possessed the lamps, only the wise had enough oil. Many people have tried to figure out what the oil is. Despite what's in the lamp, one thing stands out. Only those with filled lamps were taken up.

The bride and the five wise virgins are a type of people that seek and search for more intimacy with their Lord. Those who hunger and thirst shall be filled. Their lamps were filled because of their hungering.

We may need to rethink some of our eschatology. Several different times Jesus gives a warning to the Church to be ready for His coming. Traditionally, the Church has hoped that a simple little prayer would prepare them for the second coming of the Lord. The Church has taught many interesting things regarding this issue. It has often proclaimed that if a person said, "Jesus, come into my life and forgive me of my sins," they were ready. Consider the words at the end of Christ's teaching about the ten virgins:

> Be on the alert then, for you do not know
> the day nor the hour (Matt. 25:13).

At least three other times Jesus tells the Church to be on the alert concerning the day of His return. It does not make sense for Jesus to warn us about His coming if praying a simple prayer at one time in our lives prepares us. According to our eschatology, it is completely illogical for Jesus to tell the Church to get ready for His appearing. What is the purpose of a warning if it is not needed? Is it possible that Jesus has not made a mistake and that we have? Is it possible that God wants us to take the return of His Son quite seriously? Suppose He is trying to teach us that if we are truly Christian we will live ready, and that only the non-Christian lives unready?

It's entirely possible that we do not fully understand His return or that we use the term "Christian" too loosely. It seems that today we are giving the name "Christian" to everything and anything. Is it possible that some of the things being referred to as "Christian" might just not be? Is it possible that Jesus knew exactly what He was doing when he warned the "Church" to get ready for His return? In the parable of the ten virgins, those who were "taken-up" with Him at His return were those who were "taken-up" with Him before His return.

NOT YOUR WILL BUT MINE!

I was just going out the door of my house when the phone rang. As I answered it, I found a distraught woman on the other end calling for counsel concerning her marriage. She told me that her husband had decided to leave her and that he was leaving the very next day. This would make the failure of her third marriage.

She called me because she had just finished reading my book, *Prayer Can Change Your Marriage*. Though she said she liked the book, she was wondering if there was something else she could do to keep her husband from leaving. She was looking for a magical prayer that she could pray that would keep him from leaving her.

We talked for a little while but when she hung up the

phone, she was quite disappointed in my counsel. She was looking for a "quick fix" while I was talking about principles of prayer that take time. She wanted me to give her a formula-type prayer that would control her husband and keep him from leaving. This is why we had a conflict — she was wanting to manipulate *him* through prayer while I was talking about God changing *her* through prayer.

HOW DID JESUS PRAY?

I was talking to my close friend Dean Niforatos about how we often try to manipulate others in our prayers when he said, "I think many Christians use white magic in their prayers."

I said, "What do you mean?"

He responded, "Often I hear Christians praying for God to cause people to do certain things. They will say, 'God, make them do this or make them do that.' That is white magic!"

Is it possible that we are trying to control the lives of other people through our praying? We should be allowing God to control our lives, through our praying.

If we take a close look at the prayers of our Savior, we find that He never did pray for God to manipulate another person. One of His most famous prayers is found in Luke 22:41-42:

> And He withdrew from them about a stone's throw, and He knelt down and {began} to pray, saying, "Father, if Thou art willing, remove this cup from Me; yet not My will, but Thine be done."

Though Jesus was facing the torture of the cross and the end of His earthly life, He prayed that God would change Him, not others. Jesus knew that God causes change in others through the changes the pray-er allows God to make in his own life.

It seems that there are two basic types of pray-ers today. There are those who pray for God to change them and then there are those who pray for God to change others. The question must be asked here, "Is not praying for others a good thing?" The answer to that question is that it depends on what you are praying. If you are praying for the will of the other person to come under the will of God, then that is right and proper. If however, you are praying for God to manipulate the other person so you can get your way then there is a problem.

Jesus knew that God's ability to work in the lives of others was dependent upon His obedience to God. What would have happened if Jesus had been disobedient to God and yet continued to pray for God to cause us to do certain things? Suppose Jesus would have sinned and yet prayed for God to cause us to "see" our sin so that we would turn from it. Would the world have salvation available to them today if Jesus had not brought His will under the will of the Father?

The lady I was counseling over the phone was witnessing the failure of her third marriage. Obviously she had a problem in her own obedience to God, yet she was not seeking to bring her will under God's. She was wanting to somehow bring her husband's will under God's.

Jesus was introducing a principle to us in how He prayed. The principle is this: God works most effectively in the lives of others through the willingness of the prayer to conform to Him. Mom and Dad, do you want God to change your children? If so, bring your will under God's. Husbands and wives, do you want God to work in the lives of your mates? If so, bring your will under God's. Exercising our will is not what is important — exercising God's will is. Can you rest in God's will?

The lady on the phone was in such a panic that she was not even considering God's will concerning her own obedience to Him. She wanted her will concerning her husband. She was seeking a way to quickly fix a problem that has apparently been around for a long time; hence, three bad marriages. If she had voiced her prayer it may have sounded like this, "Not your will Lord, but mine!"

Lest I leave you thinking that I believe she was the entire problem, I need to insert something here. It's very possible that she has had three bad husbands. If so, the solution is still not in manipulating them. The answer is still in her submission to Jesus. Just think of Jesus. None of us are worthy of grace, yet rather than Him praying for God to correct us, He prayed, "Not my will, but thine." God's ability to correct us comes through Christ's submission to Him.

The problem with submission is that it does not necessarily offer an instant solution. Submission develops character. All of our problems can be traced to the lack of godly character. The lady on the phone was looking for a quick fix to avoid a conflict, and yet the very conflict she was going through was meant to help her develop in God's character. Often, it seems, we will ask God to deliver us from the very thing that is necessary to bring us into His image.

Most of us face problems because of who we are. Yet when "who we are" causes us problems, we ask God to change our circumstances rather than us. Suppose God would give us the instant fix we are looking for and miraculously change our circumstances but not change us. That would mean that in a matter of time we would face the same problems again. Most of our problems come from who we are, not from who others are. Usually, the reason people are married three or four times is that they focus on changing others, or their circumstances, rather than themselves.

I need to inject here that I do not believe every failed marriage could have been saved. When we are dealing with the free will and sinful nature of individuals, there are no guarantees. Jesus lived in complete submission to God, and yet He was put to death by those who would not conform to His message. I know of many marriages where either the wife or the husband have honestly tried to do what was right, yet the mate's mind and will remained unmovable.

TWO TYPES

There are two types of people depicted in the parable of the ten virgins. There are the wise who pray for God to change them, and then there are the foolish who pray for God to change others.

In Matthew 25:6-9, we read:

> But at midnight there was a shout, "Behold, the bridegroom! Come out to meet {him"}. Then all those virgins rose, and trimmed their lamps. And the foolish said to the prudent, "Give us some of your oil, for our lamps are going out." But the prudent answered, saying, "No, there will not be enough for us and you {too;} go instead to the dealers and buy {some} for yourselves."

I find it quite interesting that when the bridegroom came the wise could not share their oil with the foolish. The foolish wanted a quick fix, but it was not available. When the foolish were faced with a test, the first thing they did was to turn to the wise and say in essence, "You need to change. You have too much oil. Give us what you have."

They could not gain what they needed by changing the wise. They had to go out and pay a price for what they needed. The foolish had to finally do what they were unwilling to do before that time. They had to change. Unfortunately for them, it was too late. By the time the foolish returned, they were not allowed to enter in.

When I receive crisis-type phone calls from people wanting God to "zap" their mates, I want to say to them, "Why did you not live ready? How is it you did not see this coming months and months ago? Now it is too late. By the time you go out and pay the price for what you need, it will be over."

I wish more than anything I could give them a prayer to pray that would "zap" their mates, but I cannot. There are some things that cannot be passed on. The foolish were instructed to go out and pay a price for what they needed.

When I hear of marriages that are falling apart, I wish I could give them some of the oil in my lamp but I cannot do that. I wish I could give them the kind of relationship I have with my wife, but I cannot do that. I have paid a price for my relationship. My wife and I have prayed and prayed for our marriage and our home. We have sought to become what God wants us to be. It is not something that came easily, it came with a price and we are still paying it.

I wish I could offer my faith to another person, but I cannot. I wish I could offer my salvation to others, but I cannot. These things can only be gained from God.

BUY FROM ME!

Because you say, "I am rich, and have become wealthy, and have need of nothing," and you do not know that you are wretched and miserable and poor and blind and naked, I advise you to buy from Me gold refined by fire, that you may become rich (Rev. 3:17–18).

The church of Laodicea had an attitude that was not spiritually healthy. Her attitude was that she had need of nothing. She did not see herself as the one who needed to change. She had an attitude similar to the Pharisee who prayed for God to change others and said, "God I am glad I am not like other men." Yet the man who prayed,

"Lord, have mercy on me," and was willing to change, was the one who found favor with God.

The Spirit of God is counseling the church of Laodicea. He is instructing her to "buy" what she needs. She must pay a price to gain what she needs. Prayer is the payment. We must pay the price of prayer long before the crisis. Prayer is the very thing that prepares us for His appearing. It seems the life of prayer is a difficult thing to develop. As much as I talk to the Church about living ready through the life of prayer it is still an unheeded message. It's as if the message cannot be heard.

The woman who called me had no oil. Her lamp was empty. The hour of testing had come to her, and she was not ready. She wanted oil from me but I could not give it to her. All I could do was instruct her to go out and buy some oil. However, by the time she could gain what she needed it most likely was too late. Her husband was leaving the next day.

PURIFICATION

Your oils have a pleasing fragrance, Your name is {like} purified oil; Therefore the maidens love you (Song of Sol. 1:3).

Verse three of the opening chapter of the "Song" contains some interesting thoughts about the oil that the maidens get from the groom. It says that not only do the maidens love the groom, but they love the oil they gain from their relationship with him. The five wise virgins from Matthew 25 were ready for the groom because of the oil in their lamps. There is an interesting parallel between the oil that prepares us for the return of Christ and oil as a cosmetic.

ESTHER

When King Ahasuerus sat on his royal throne in Susa, the capital, he reigned from India to Ethiopia over 127 provinces (see Esther 1:1). Queen Vasthi had angered him, so an edict went out to gather all the beautiful young women for the king.

> And let the king appoint overseers in all the provinces of his kingdom that they may gather every beautiful young virgin to Susa the capital, to the harem, into the custody of Hegai, the king's eunuch, who was in charge of the women; and let their cosmetics be given {them} (Esther 2:3).

This is a reference to the purification process that took place before the young women could even be brought before the king. Each of the young women was given cosmetics.

No less than 12 months was allowed them for their purification so that they might be very clean and perfumed. Even those who were the masterpieces of nature were required to go through this process of purification.

> Now when the turn of each young lady came to go in to King Ahasuerus, after the end of her twelve months under the regulations for the women — for the days of their beautification were completed as follows: six months with oil of myrrh and six months with spices and the cosmetics for women (Esther 2:12).

All this preparation seems quite extreme because we are talking about a mere man. Though he was the king of the land, he was still just a man. How is it a mere man could require such standards from other men? In the king's case we are seeing the extent of the carnal mind and the subsequent exaltation of that mind. However, if we can see the typology here, there is an application that is important for us.

A SPOTLESS BRIDE

That He might present to Himself the church in all her glory, having no spot or wrinkle or any such thing; but that she should be holy and blameless (Eph. 5:27).

Each of us, as the bride of Christ, are to be preparing ourselves to be presented before our King one day. We, too, are to be without spot or wrinkle. *It could be said that our entire life is to be a purification process.* Our whole life is to be spent preparing ourselves for that great day when we stand before Him. When we stand before the love of our life, we will want no blemish of any type.

Today we should eagerly seek the oil of the Holy Spirit for purification and cleansing. However, this oil is only available from one source, our Lord. The five wise virgins of Matthew 25 sought out this oil and paid a great price to gain it. The five foolish paid very little attention to their need. They did not seek the oil. Subsequently, they were not prepared to stand before him on that great day.

THE PREPARATION OF THE BRIDE

In Psalm 34:5 we read, "Those who look to him are radiant; their faces are never covered with shame."

We are to be constantly looking unto Him. Our radiance, or oil, comes through looking to Him. The oil we receive from our pursuit of Him is used in preparing us for His return. When He comes, those whose lamps are filled with oil will be ready. Those who hear the message of pursuing Him but never heed it, will have no radiance. They will lack the oil that can only come from Him.

I do not believe a woman's obsession with beauty comes purely from vanity. It is a God-given part of her nature. The Lord prompted me to observe my wife's attention to detail in this regard. Whenever I travel through London's Heathrow Airport, my wife makes sure I bring her a bottle of her favorite perfume. She also has a certain brand of makeup that she goes out of her way to obtain. Why is this? Why is it men seem to always have to wait for their wives to get ready to go out? It's because they are teaching, by example, the diligence the Church is to have in its preparation for the return of her Groom. The woman, by nature, wants to be attractive.

The Church should be just as diligent in her prayer and preparation as a woman is in her oils and cosmetics. A church that does not pray would be like a woman that gives no attention to these matters. A prayerless church represents a woman that does not concern herself with her own attraction. Those who look to the Lord become radiant. A prayerless church has no attraction, no radiance. Therefore, there is no outward appeal to the groom or the sinner.

COME, LORD JESUS!

And the Spirit and the bride say, "Come."
And let the one who hears say, "Come" (Rev. 22:17).

Each of us should be living with a great desire for Jesus to return. Our prayer lives reflect our desire for Him.

I once preached a message about the return of Jesus. In my message, I talked about living ready because no man knows the day or the hour of His return. I preached from the perspective that Jesus could come at any minute. The next day I received a phone call from a very angry woman who was in the service the night before. She said I had no right preaching about the return of Christ. I told her that I was not date setting. I was not trying to predict when He would return. I was simply warning the church so that she would live ready. She remained very upset over the fact that I "scared" people into thinking that He could return soon.

It really did not make any sense to me about why she was struggling with this subject until about two months later. It turned out she was involved in an affair and left her husband and children for another man. In other words, she was not living ready and did not like the idea of His return. The wise live ready, the foolish do not. Those who live ready long for the return of Christ. The Spirit of God within them cries out for the return of the Son of God and says, "Come, Lord Jesus!"

LUKEWARM!

I was in the midst of a three-day solemn assembly once when a very interesting thing happened. We had been fasting for three days as a church. Every day we would gather at 6:00 a.m. and stay until 10:00 p.m. The days were filled with prayer, reading the Word, worship and teaching. Often throughout the day people would give testimonies of what God was doing in their lives. Most of the people felt free to express the struggles they were going through in their relationship with God. Some did not.

On the evening of the final night, a young mom came to the microphone. As she stood there, tears began to well up in her eyes. She slowly began to share with us what had happened to her the previous evening at her home. She told us how she had been present for much of the solemn assembly. However, she did not really feel she needed to do anything about her relationship with God (typical daughter of Zion attitude). She felt no need to repent of anything like the others were doing. She was the wife of a very successful man with a beautiful new home. She also had two lovely young children. That night something was different. She had trouble sleeping. As the night progressed she became more restless. Suddenly, in the middle of the night, her young daughter became sick. As she tended her daughter she knew that her daughter was about to "lose her supper." As she attempted to get her daughter to the bathroom it was too late. She threw up all over the hallway. She cleaned her daughter up and put her back to bed. She was fine now. Then she went to clean up the hallway. As she got down on her knees with a wash cloth in her hand God began to speak to her. As she wiped up the "mess" God spoke to her and said, "Lukewarm." At this point during her testimony she was weeping quite openly. She cried, "What did you say?"

God spoke to her again and said, "You are lukewarm."

She said, "What do you mean?"

God responded by saying, "I will vomit you out of my mouth just as your daughter vomited out her dinner."

> So because you are lukewarm, and neither hot nor cold, I will vomit you out of My mouth (Rev. 3:16;NKJV).

She then said, "God had to get me with my face to the floor, knee-deep in vomit, before I could hear Him say that I had become to Him like the vomit I was cleaning up." After this testimony the entire church was weeping as God examined each of our lives.

THEY WON'T COME!

Shortly after I was saved, our church was going to participate in a retreat for the college-aged people. I was very excited about this! I did not know many young people in our church so I looked at this as a great opportunity to meet them.

I stopped in to talk to my pastor about this and said to him, "This retreat is going to be a wonderful time. I am looking forward to being with the others from our church."

He looked at me and said, "I would not get too excited about meeting very many from our church."

I said, "Why not?"

He said, "You will not understand this yet because you are a new Christian, but those who go to this retreat will be those who have gotten saved recently. Those who have grown up in the church simply will not be interested in going."

He was right. Only a handful came from our church. This began to break my heart. I just could not understand why people would lose their love for Jesus, but they do! It's called "lukewarmness." Do not be foolish. Be wise! Seek his face. Renew your first love. Enter into the secret place and give yourself to Him. Let Him see your form. Let Him hear your voice. Bathe yourself in the oil that comes from Him. Stand ready for His appearing without spot or wrinkle.

The message of this book can be summed up with one word — "pray." Spend more and more time in His presence. He will take care of the rest.

THE CHURCH, THE BRIDE

There seems to be a considerable amount of controversy over who the Bride is. Some say that the Church cannot be the Bride because the Bride is the New Jerusalem that comes down from heaven in the Book of Revelation. While Revelation does refer to the New Jerusalem as the bride of Christ, that does not conflict in any way with the idea of the Church being the Bride today. In fact, the Bible seems to suggest that the Church is both the Bride and the New Jerusalem.

The Song of Solomon teaches us that the Bride is the place where the King reigns. Today Jesus reigns in the heart of His believers. These believers are also known as the Church. The kingdom of God on earth is within the heart of the regenerate man. If all men on earth were Christians, this would be the kingdom of God because Satan would have no rule at all. God would reign throughout the land just as He wants to do within us now.

The "Kingdom now" or "dominion theology" is, in part, why there is a controversy over who the bride of Christ is. "Kingdom now" theology teaches that we are to be preparing the earth for the return of Christ. They do not believe in any kind of rapture of the Church. It teaches that Jesus will come back when we have successfully prepared a dwelling place for Him here on earth. Most of the current spiritual warfare teaching follows this reasoning. This is why it has become so militant. This is also why we have had such a strong emphasis on "taking our cities for God." They do not have a sound focus on saving individuals but on driving evil from the earth. It is their belief that Jesus will not come back until the evil is gone. E.M. Bounds once said, "You cannot save a city. Cities cannot give themselves to Christ. You can only save individuals."

Jesus addressed this whole issue of His kingdom with the Pharisees.

> Once, having been asked by the Pharisees when the kingdom of God would come, Jesus replied, "The kingdom of God does not come with your careful observation, nor will people say, 'Here it is,' or 'There it is,' because the kingdom of God is within you" (Luke 17:20–21).

They were looking for a physical kingdom. They were hoping for positions of power.

Jesus must have burst their bubble when He said, in essence, "You guys have it all wrong. The kingdom of God is spiritual and it does not have positions of power but humility." In the current "Kingdom now" teaching there is a great emphasis on the "manifest sons of God." They will supposedly be men that God will raise up with tremendous power and authority. These men will reign with God, not under God, but with God. They are looking for the kingdom of God to come as a physical structure in which they will have positions of power. The promoters of this theory are modern-day Pharisees who have corrupted our current religious order.

THE NEW JERUSALEM

Revelation teaches us that one day the New Jerusalem will come down from heaven:

> And I saw the holy city, new Jerusalem, coming down out of heaven from God, made ready as a bride adorned for her husband (Rev. 21:2).

The New Jerusalem is going to be the place from which Christ will govern on earth. The heart of the Bride is the place where Christ governs from today. Does Jesus have a throne on earth today? Yes! It's the heart of His Bride. Confusion can come in when we try to explain what the New Jerusalem is really made of. I do not believe this is something any man can understand fully because the Bible is not fully clear on it. All we really know is that it is where Christ will dwell.

> And I saw no temple in it, for the Lord God, the Almighty, and the Lamb, are its temple. And the city has no need of the sun or of the moon to shine upon it, for the glory of God has illumined it, and its lamp [is] the Lamb (Rev. 21:22–23).

How do we explain a city where God will reign that has no temple in it? This can be as confusing to us as believers as it is to a nonbeliever when we tell them that God dwells in our hearts today. The Bible says we are the temple of God, but we do not have a physical temple within us. What we have is a heart. When we say God dwells in our heart, do we mean that literally? Do we mean to say that God has physically reduced himself down to a size that will fit inside our flesh and blood hearts? No! What believers mean to say is that God has become our essence, our heart. God has come into our lives and now guides our thoughts, actions, and emotions.

The "Kingdom now" theory believes that the

"manifest sons of God" will ultimately rule with Christ as equals. They struggle with the idea that they are the Bride. They want to be kings. If the Church is the Bride that would put them in a subordinate position. From their perspective it would be better to be king than queen. We must understand that the "Kingdom now" theology was born out of pride. It uses Revelation's description of the New Jerusalem as proof that the Church cannot be the Bride because it describes the Bride as a city.

> And the city is laid out as a square, and its length is as great as the width; and he measured the city with the rod, fifteen hundred miles; its length and width and height are equal (Rev. 21:16).

While it is true that this is a physical description, how do we deal with Solomon's description of his bride? In the Song of Songs 7:4, Solomon is sweet-talking his bride:

> Your neck is like a tower of ivory, your eyes [like] the pools in Heshbon by the gate of Bathrabbim; your nose is like the tower of Lebanon, which faces toward Damascus.

Solomon is describing his bride as his kingdom. How romantic would it be to be lying next to your wife in bed and say, "Honey, your nose is like the tower of Lebanon." That is probably not going to get a cuddly response from your wife. Obviously, Solomon did not mean it in a literal sense, but in a figurative sense. The king was looking at his bride as his dwelling place, as his kingdom. The bride houses the kingdom.

> Your neck is like the tower of David built with rows of stones (Song of Sol. 4:4).

Solomon describes the neck of his bride as a tower built of stones. Does he mean this literally? Or is he attributing to her qualities that are similar to a city? What we begin to see in this is that it's possible that the New Jerusalem is both a city and the Bride.

HIS BRIDE

Throughout the New Testament the Church is referred to as the Bride. The Book of Ephesians probably brings this out better than any other:

> For the husband is the head of the wife, as Christ also is the head of the church, He Himself [being] the Savior of the body. But as the church is subject to Christ, so also the wives [ought to be] to their husbands in everything (Eph. 5:23–24).

The husband is the head of the wife, his bride, just as Christ is the head of the Church, His Bride. The Church as the Bride is to be subject to Christ, its head, in the same way that the wife is to be subject to her husband. A man's wife is his kingdom. A man cannot be a husband if he has no wife. Or you could say, "A man cannot be a king if he has no queen."

> Husbands, love your wives, just as Christ also loved the church and gave Himself up for her; that He might sanctify her, having cleansed her by the washing of water with the word, that He might present to Himself the church in all her glory, having no spot or wrinkle or any such thing; but that she should be holy and blameless (Eph. 5:25–27).

One day Jesus is going to present to himself His Bride, the Church. Do we believe Jesus is going to be married to a city? Isn't it interesting to think that some people want to interpret the city in Revelation as a literal, physical city having nothing to do with the Church and yet when that is carried out to it's fullest extent, it would also be saying that Jesus' Bride is a city.

Jesus' Bride is where He reigns. Is it possible that the New Jerusalem is the Church? Could it be possible that somehow what the Revelator saw was the Church in all her glory coming down as the Bride, the dwelling place for God on earth?

John the Revelator described the walls of the city as precious stones. In Revelation 21:18-21 we read:

> And the material of the wall was jasper; and the city was pure gold, like clear glass. The foundation stones of the city wall were adorned with every kind of precious stone. The first foundation stone was jasper; the second, sapphire; the third, chalcedony; the fourth, emerald; the fifth, sardonyx; the sixth, sardius; the seventh, chrysolite; the eighth, beryl; the ninth, topaz; the tenth, chrysoprase; the eleventh, jacinth; the twelfth, amethyst. And the twelve gates were twelve pearls; each one of the gates was a single pearl. And the street of the city was pure gold, like transparent glass (Rev. 21:18–21).

Consider Revelation's description of the city walls as stones, to Peter's statement in 1 Peter 2:5:

> You also, as living stones, are being built up as a spiritual house for a holy priesthood, to offer up spiritual sacrifices acceptable to God through Jesus Christ.

Does Peter mean we human beings are going to turn into a house? Are we going to become a physical house made of precious stones and rocks? Did Solomon actually mean that his bride's neck was made of stones? Is it possible that the precious stones which make up the walls of the New Jerusalem are the righteous acts of the saints? In Revelation 21:2, we read how the city had been made ready as a bride. The city was adorned in a wedding garment. The garment the bride wears will be made up of the righteous acts she (the Church) did while on earth.

> And it was given to her to clothe herself in
> fine linen, bright [and] clean; for the fine linen is
> the righteous acts of the saints (Rev. 19:8).

The fine linen describes the wedding gown. This gown is without spot or wrinkle because it is made up of the righteous acts of the saints. The saints, who make up the Church, performed righteous acts while on earth. These acts literally become her gown. This is why 1 Corinthians uses precious stones as a description of good works during the judgement seat of Christ.

> Now if any man builds upon the founda-
> tion with gold, silver, precious stones, wood, hay,
> straw, each man's work will become evident; for
> the day will show it, because it is [to be] revealed
> with fire; and the fire itself will test the quality
> of each man's work (1 Cor. 3:12–13).

Could it be that every righteous act we do today is laying the foundation for the New Jerusalem? These acts are creating the walls for the dwelling place for God on earth. Is it possible that these righteous acts (precious stones) give the wedding gown its glow and glory? What the Revelator may have seen is the Church coming down as the New Jerusalem, the dwelling place for God. She was clothed in her wedding garment (her righteous acts while on earth), which make up the walls and foundation of the city.

I GO TO PREPARE A PLACE

In My Father's house are many dwelling places; if it were not so, I would have told you; for I go to prepare a place for you. And if I go and prepare a place for you, I will come again, and receive you to Myself; that where I am, [there] you may be also (John 14:2–3).

Jesus refers to His Father's house in a singular sense. God has one house with many dwelling places. Could this be the city John the Revelator sees coming down from heaven?

We should probably rethink some things about heaven. For many years I have heard Christians talk about Jesus building each of us a mansion in heaven. When you think about it, it does not make sense for Him to do that. We refer to heaven as our eternal resting place. That really is not consistent with Scripture. It's true that if you were to die today you would go to be present with the Lord. However, you would only stay in that state (heaven) until the day of the Lord.

When Jesus comes to dwell on earth during the Millennium, the Church comes with Him to reign with Him:

And Thou hast made them [to be] a kingdom and priests to our God; and they will reign upon the earth (Rev. 5:10).

Here again we see the Church as both a kingdom (the dwelling place for God) and priests (rulers). It seems that from this point on, we will never dwell in heaven again. The earth becomes our eternal home.

The Great White Throne Judgement follows the millennial reign (see Rev. 20:10–15). The New Jerusalem comes down from heaven after the great judgement when Satan is bound forever and thrown into the lake of fire.

Jesus is preparing a place for us within the city itself. However, whether it is a literal dwelling place or not is not clear. After the city comes down from heaven, we will serve the Lord forever. Revelation 22:3 brings this out:

> And there shall no longer be any curse; and the throne of God and of the Lamb shall be in it, and His bond-servants shall serve Him.

The "place" that is being prepared for us could be twofold. It could be a literal place to live and a position of servanthood within the kingdom. Don't we each have a place right now within the kingdom of God? Don't we each have opportunities to serve God today? Is not our serving, our place right now?

Is the Church the bride of Christ? Certainly! Is the Church the New Jerusalem? Certainly! There is no conflict. She is both. Do I understand how she could be both? No! But I do not understand how the Trinity could be three-in-one and one-in-three, either. I do not understand how Jesus could live in me now. I do not understand divine healing other than it being a miracle. Maybe that is it — it's a miracle. It is something we do not need to fully understand because our God is in charge of it.

ENDNOTES

Introduction
1 Delmer Guynes, *Queen of the Realm* (Kuala Lumpur, Malaysia: Calvary Church Press, 1986), p. 1–2.
2 Ibid., p. 2.
3 Thomas Dehany Bernard, *The Progress of Doctrine in the New Testament* (London: Pickering & Inglis, 1968), p. 170.
4 Guynes, *Queen of the Realm*, p. 4.
5 Ibid., p. 5.

Chapter 1
1 Guynes, *Queen of the Realm*, p. 3–4.
2 Ibid., p. 9.
3 Ibid., p. 10.

Chapter 3
1 Guynes, *Queen of the Realm*, p. 17–18.

Chapter 7
1 Guynes, *Queen of the Realm*, p. 93.
2 Ibid.

Chapter 8
1 Wade Taylor, *The Secret of the Stairs* (Salisbury Center, NY: Pinecrest Publications, 1988), p. 26.

Chapter 10
1 *Matthew Henry's Commentary on the Whole Bible: New Modern Edition,* electronic database, Hendrickson Publishers, Inc., 1991.

Also by Ron Auch

Unshakable Man
A Stable Spiritual Force in the Home

The Bible says that the world needs men who will take heaven by force. That doesn't mean assaulting the Word of God and His Holiness. In fact, it means quite the opposite: This world is so vile and doomed that families are desperate for fathers and husbands who will pledge themselves to be committed warriors for truth.

Written especially for men who have a serious inner desire to be better in every area of their lives, this is not a book for those interested in casual or effortless change. Some change is hard, but the benefits are far-reaching. Auch implores men to arrive at a place of better living by paying strict attention to their responsibilities: families, marriages, and careers.

ISBN: 0-89221-323-X • 162 pages • $9.95

Available at Christian bookstores nationwide

Also by Ron Auch

The Heart of the King

A Devotional
Commentary on
Psalm 119

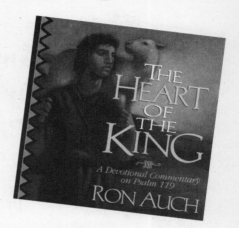

Do we know anymore what it means to
yearn for God? Do our hearts ache to spend time with
Him? Author Ron Auch explores the intense relationship
between God and His famous servant King David, as
chronicled in the 176 verses of Psalm 119. It's not enough
to just pray a few minutes each week; *The Heart of the
King* illustrates convincingly that "the man after God's own
heart" had a heart for Him.

Auch captures the mood of King David with a commentary after each verse, and challenges the reader that
although world-changing leaders like David are rare, each
human can have that same oneness with God.

Elegant in design, and having a substantive text, this
casebound book will make an excellent gift and rich addi-
tion to anyone's collection.

ISBN: 0-89221-278-0 • 192 pages • $12.95 • casebound

Available at Christian bookstores nationwide

Also by Ron Auch

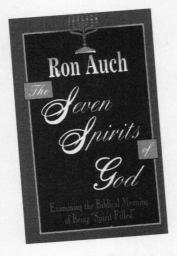

The Seven Spirits of God

The seven Spirits of God are mentioned four times in the Book of Revelation. What are they and how do they pertain to us?

The seven Spirits of God detail the biblical meaning of being "Spirit filled." God has a definite purpose in wanting His Spirit to dwell within men. Peter defined it when he said, "You may participate in the (His) divine nature and escape the corruption of the world." The Spirit of God is to help us overcome the impurity of this world. This book challenges its readers to examine themselves to see if they emulate all of the fullness of God and are truly living the overcomer's life.

ISBN: 0-89221-238-1 • 192 pages • $9.95
Leader's Guide: ISBN 0-89221-274-8 • 60 pages • $4.50

Available at Christian bookstores nationwide

Also by Ron Auch

He Hears Your Prayers

The culmination of almost 20 years of a nationally respected prayer ministry, *He Hears Your Prayers* makes a vital prayer life within the grasp of everyone.

Author and seminar speaker Ron Auch provides a simple, workable plan for building a prayer life in the everyday experience of believers. Auch takes an elementary approach to prayer, allowing the reader to first look at how to pray, then progressing to more complex steps such as intercessory prayer.

Based on his popular lecture series, this book isn't content with explaining how to pray, but with debunking commonly held myths and developing life-long prayer and communication with God.

ISBN: 0-89221-423-6 • 160 pages • $10.99

Available at Christian bookstores nationwide

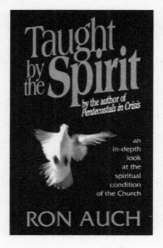